D0231738

FALL OUT

Also by Janet Street-Porter:

Baggage

FALL OUT

Janet Street-Porter

All images belong to the author. Thanks to Tim Street-Porter for his photographs. Waitress and Hatstand images copyright Allen Jones

First published in 2006 by Headline Review
a division of the HEADLINE PUBLISHING GROUP

1

Cataloguing in Publication Data is available
from the British Library

ISBN-10 0 7553 1495 6
ISBN-13 978 07553 1495 9

Typeset in Perpetua by Avon DataSet Ltd,
Bidford on Avon, Warwickshire

Printed and bound in Great Britain by
Mackays of Chatham plc, Chatham, Kent

Headline's policy is to use papers that are natural, renewable and recyclable products and made from wood grown in sustainable forests. The logging and manufacturing processes are expected to conform to the environmental regulations of the country of origin.

Every effort has been made to fulfil requirements with regard to reproducing copyright material. The author and publisher will be glad to rectify any omissions at the earliest opportunity.

HEADLINE PUBLISHING GROUP
A division of Hodder Headline
338 Euston Road
Lonon NW1 3BH

www.reviewbooks.co.uk
www.hodderheadline.com

For Pat

Contents

Introduction

How many friends do you really need? As many as fill an address book? As many as you can count on the fingers of two hands? If you've grown up with the kind of parents I had, then your friends are your family. But friendship isn't like a blood relationship, it morphs and changes according to the times. Friends are conduits to exploring the moment to the full, they take you places you would never have got to alone . . . and then the time arrives when friends become baggage, and the painful process starts of gradually shedding them to make room for new acquaintances, new experiences, new challenges and new delights to enjoy. You can call me ruthless, driven, single-minded, self-centred – and you'd be right. My journey through life has encompassed newspapers, television, radio, the art world and the theatre. I've been married many times, lived with people almost continuously from the age of 18 when I first ran away from home. Along the way I've had intense relationships with like-minded people, and then I've moved on. They are the enablers, who provided me with access all areas in their particular field – and then, just as swiftly as I needed to know them, I reluctantly discard them. There's the guilt to live with, but nothing ever stops the inevitable process.

In a cupboard in my house sits a box of address books, going back forty years. Some are small leather pocket affairs, one is printed with flowers, others are well-thumbed black leather Filofaxes. One slim volume is embossed with the swirling Biba logo in gold, while another red silk book is emblazoned with Wonder Woman. The contents of each is subtly different from its predecessor. Year after year I laboriously copied the names from one full book to the next, and if I happened to have lost one, then I started a new book from scratch. Each volume is the key to unlocking my life at a particular time, for it holds the names of the lovers, the work mates, the best friends, the confidants, the people who came to dinner. When a book fell apart from overuse, I started another, and in the act of beginning at A time after time, I would consciously edit out a few people to make room for new information, new friends. So what happened to the names that never made it? This book is about the fallout, the important people who got airbrushed out, my way of recognising the part they played in making me the person I am today.

I left home at 19, having cancelled my forthcoming wedding to the man I had been engaged to for two years. I moved in with my lover, who I would later marry, and together we threw away our years of architectural training. Tim became a highly successful photographer working for the glossy magazines, and I started a career as a journalist. By the age of 22 I had a weekly column in a national newspaper. Over the next decade I would be at the centre of the art and music scene in London night after night, backstage with Pink Floyd, drinking with Janis Joplin. I'd model for Zandra Rhodes and put on a show at Joan Littlewood's theatre at Stratford East. I'd meet Barbara Hulaniki, Twiggy, Manolo Blahnik and Ossie Clark would design my wedding dress. I'd get busted for drugs and go on anti-war demonstrations.

I'd have lunch with Terence Stamp and spend hours in drinking clubs with Francis Bacon. I was a strange mixture of brash exterior and insecure interior. My hair changed colour about as often as I had sex. I tried owning pets, but they didn't last much longer than the husbands. The decade started with the Rolling Stones and ended with Johnny Rotten. It was inevitable there would be fallout.

Chapter 1

The morning after my wedding party, I dripped around the flat with a hangover, trying to tidy up the mess. I gathered together the spliffs and acid tabs and popped them in a brown envelope on which I helpfully wrote the word 'DRUGS!' in black Pentel. I got the 1950's nudie 16mm movie and a couple of underground comics we'd been given and stuffed them in another big envelope and wrote 'PORN!' on it as a joke. I put both envelopes in a prominent position on the shelf in our office, to be dealt with on our return. Only the heart-shaped layer of the cake had been eaten, so I found a tin and put the large square layer in it – I'd send it off to the relatives later. Then I stuffed a bag with sweaters and jeans, got some scarves, cameras, tapes and hats, said goodbye to George, the lodger, and set off in the car on our honeymoon. Our destination was the artist Patrick Heron's house high up on the moors above Zennor in Cornwall, between St Ives and Land's End.

I'd resumed communications with my parents about two weeks earlier after months of silence. I'd walked out of their semi-d in dreary Perivale in west London one Friday night in January 1967, leaving in a tantrum without money or clothes (I sneaked back there a couple of days later while they were out at work, and took bags of my stuff, my books and records). They were livid when they discovered I was sharing a room in a huge flat in Earls Court with Tim. Later we moved into a flat in Hereford House, a mansion block on Fulham Road, near Chelsea football ground, but my mother managed to find the address and they appeared at the door one Saturday, demanding I go home. I refused, and my father started shouting that he would make me a ward of court. I slammed the door in his face, but I was very unsettled that my relationship with my parents had deteriorated so much, and I was frightened that they might somehow take me away from Tim. They were furious that I was neglecting my studies – understandable, I suppose – but my relationship with Tim had totally taken over my life. I was 20 years old, and Mum and Dad could no longer control what I did, any more than they could control what I wore or how I did my hair.

I was totally infatuated with Tim. He was tall, thin, good-looking, interested in the same music, art and movies as me – Jean-Luc Godard, Pink Floyd, Robert Rauschenberg, art deco and cutting-edge design. Tim had studied architecture in London, and then spent two years in San Francisco working as an assistant to a practice in Berkeley. It was at the height of counter-culture, with violent student demonstrations, and San Francisco was the spiritual home of flower power, with the Avalon Ballroom and underground bookshops where there were regular poetry readings by people like Alan Ginsburg. Tim was very English and charming, with a pronounced stammer and an upper middle class accent, and he soon fell in with a whole group of interesting artists and musicians, from Country Joe and the Fish to Janis Joplin and Big Brother and the Holding Company.

Some of his friends stayed with us in the following months and years, en route to asylum and a refuge in Sweden, fleeing the draft and the prospect of fighting in

Vietnam in a war they violently opposed. Tim had only returned to England in 1966 because he, too, had been called up, and although the authorities had let him go he had been told he might not be so lucky if he was drafted a second time. He decided it was too risky so he had come back home, and he decided within three months to abandon his architectural studies in his final year (his father was absolutely furious) at Regent Street Polytechnic and work as a trainee film editor, picking up photographic commissions whenever he could. Soon he was regularly working for the architectural press, and learning how to edit TV commercials. He'd already shot and cut his own films of Las Vegas and California on Super-8, and they'd been shown at the Institute of Contemporary Arts in the Mall, which is how we'd met.

Two weeks before the marriage ceremony, we organised a dinner so that both sets of parents could meet, at the 555 Bistro in Battersea, a small unpretentious place with red and white check tablecloths and a temperamental Polish chef/patron.

A year before, when I'd called off my wedding to my long-suffering fiancé Rex (another architect) shortly after meeting Tim, my mother had declared to anyone who'd listen, 'I've never felt so ashamed in my life. I simply can't hold up my head when I walk down the street.' Now, when I rang to invite Mum and Dad to the dinner, she launched into a tirade about my morality, my desire to shame the family. Nevertheless, my parents eventually agreed to meet the Street-Porters, and to everyone's relief the evening was a success and all four got on famously.

Tim's dad, Cecil, was a Lloyd's underwriter (in fact, he was on the board of Lloyd's) who specialised in expeditions. Cecil's family had lost all their money and their grand house in Suffolk during the 1920s, but he had been educated at public school, and seemed (to me) rather formal and quite intimidating. He was a keen bird-watcher, and passionate about the countryside. Tim and I had spent some happy weekends at the family farmhouse outside Tregaron in mid-Wales. It was always freezing outside high summer and very basically furnished – very much the Street-Porter style. Tim's mother, Marjorie, was a miner's daughter, but you would never know it. She had come to London from the north and she had met Cecil at the florist shop where she worked in Sloane Street, Belgravia. Her accent was extremely correct, all regionality firmly repressed.

They lived in a double-fronted Georgian house in the highly desirable Pond Road, just off Blackheath in south-east London. The living room had a few pieces of fine period furniture, and there was a blue plaque by their front door which read 'Nathaniel Hawthorne, author, lived here'. I was impressed. Both Street-Porter parents were mad keen on economy living, and hated waste and ostentation.

My father was by now an electrical engineer for the London Borough of Brent. I had already embarrassed him eighteen months earlier, when he got me a holiday job as an architectural assistant in his offices and I turned up for work in a silver PVC miniskirt with matching coat, and spent three weeks designing a sports centre in a blow-up dome rather than a conventional building. He was mortified, and extremely relieved when my employment came to an end. My mother had lied about her qualifications to land a job as a clerical assistant in the Holland Park tax office. She, too, had roped me in as holiday relief one Christmas, and I'd blotted my copybook by taking over the switchboard one morning and disconnecting everyone constantly. I was also caught reading the files of the famous in the toilets when I should have been putting them back on the shelves. Mind you, I had been made to sign the Official Secrets Act before taking up my post.

Tim and I realised that our wedding plans had to accommodate our parents' wishes, so we booked a room at the Terrazza, the most fashionable Italian restaurant in Soho, for a family lunch after the ceremony. The 'Trat', as it was known, was synonymous with swinging London, always cropping up in the gossip columns as the haunt of pop stars and actors. Our event was to be a bit more sedate, a sit-down lunch in a private room, the guest list decided by our parents – about twenty members of our immediate families in all.

Meanwhile, Tim and I commissioned Piers Gough, who had been my best buddy when I was at college at the Architectural Association, to design our personal invite to our wedding party, which we mailed out to our friends. It was printed on thin pink paper and was a drawing of Tim sitting in front of the piano in our kitchen, with the cat on the keyboard and me framed in a photo on the lid. It was subsequently printed in the *Guardian* in a feature about fashionable wedding invitations! We asked about a hundred people to 'join us in our marital bliss' and come to a bash at our flat in the evening. The guest list was a varied group of designers, architects, photographers and musicians – from Zandra

Janet & Timothy Street-Porter invite you to inspect them in their married bliss and join them on their first night together at nine oclock on the eleventh of November
22 Hereford House Fulham Road SW10

Rhodes and her boyfriend, Alex McIntyre, to my ex-lover the artist Joe Tilson and his wife, Molly Parkin (then fashion editor of *Nova* magazine), and of course many of our friends from college. It was going to be a brilliant night.

Ossie Clark was making my wedding dress. The truth is, I didn't really like it, but I was too scared to tell him. Ossie was so fashionable, the hottest designer of the moment, with his shop Quorum on Radnor Walk, just off the Kings Road. His business partner and fellow designer, Alice Pollock, was married to a great friend of Tim, but Ossie was undoubtedly the star designer in the partnership. We had been to many of Ossie's parties, the most memorable of which was his birthday party, held at the Revolution Club in Mayfair earlier in 1967. Ike and Tina Turner played, to about a hundred people.

To our astonishment John Lennon turned up with a dumpy Japanese woman who wore no makeup and had long, bushy dark hair and pronounced eyebrows – she looked totally out of place among all the stick-thin models with short skirts and blond hair. It later emerged this was the avant-garde artist Yoko Ono – John had met her at the Indica gallery in the West End in November 1966, and was infatuated with her, even though he was married to Cynthia and had a son, Julian. I was six foot tall and as skinny as anything, in spite of eating a massive amount. To me, the idea that he could fancy a short thing like Yoko was incredible.

Ossie's dress was in soft lavender crepe, with a long skirt and huge pleated lace collar and cuffs. I thought it looked like a couture version of the horrible overall I'd had to wear when I worked in Woolworths all those years ago, but Ossie was so temperamental that I didn't dare say anything – especially as he was giving it me as a present. Tim had decided to wear a pinstriped suit with a long, narrow, double-breasted jacket and skinny trousers, from Just Men (a boutique off the Kings Road), teamed with a Michael Fish shirt.

A week before the wedding Tim and I had the idea of putting hash into one of the layers of the wedding cake I was going to bake. It was a two-tier job, constructed out of fruit cake – I had purchased columns to stand it all up. There was to be a square layer at the bottom for the relatives, which would be cut up and sent out in boxes to those not invited or living far away. A heart-shaped cake

on the top would contain grated dope to enliven our evening knees-up. One Friday night I mixed a giant amount of fruit cake in a large bowl on the table in the kitchen, watched by Tim and George Marsden, our lodger.

George had moved in during the summer of 1967, when I hadn't got a job – except for a bit of waitressing at lunchtimes – and Tim was on a lowly trainee film editor's pay. He was a friend of one of the girls who lived in the flat upstairs (also a teacher), and was an amenable blond chap in his twenties, who taught Latin at a comprehensive school in west London. He used to regale me with stories of finding the gardener at the school puffing on a spliff – it seems he'd been growing some plants in the greenhouse. Both George and Tim smoked dope quite regularly, but as I'd never acquired any craving for cigarettes as a schoolgirl (I couldn't stand the taste of tobacco and hated inhaling the stuff) I often just ate bits of it in hash cookies.

We waited for the dealer to show up. In fact, we waited for about five hours and then, furious that our plans had been ruined, I just spooned the mixture into the tins and stuck it in the oven. The bloke actually rang the doorbell the next night, but by then it was too late, and the hash got smoked by Tim and George while I endeavoured to cover my extravagant cake tower in icing. Where it looked a bit messy, I covered the blobs with sugared almonds, and finished the whole thing off with a little plastic bride and groom – perfect!

The day of the wedding went like these things generally do, full of anxious moments interspersed with black comedy. First thing in the morning I rushed off to the hairdresser, Harold Leighton on Conduit Street (considered one of the most fashionable in London), who decided to turn my normally straight hair into a series of backcombed arcs. I thought it looked frightful, but Harold was very pleased with his work. (I have never looked like this ever again – it really was a once-in-a-lifetime coiffure!) Back home I gritted my teeth and put on the unflattering mauve coverall designed by Ossie, and soon my father arrived to pick me up from our flat. Tim went to the Chelsea register office with his father in another car – they seemed to think it was bad form for us to arrive together, even though we lived just down the road from the building. Outside the register office, my father pulled up, and he was so nervous that he managed to slam the car door shut on my leg. I limped past a sign that said 'London Borough of Chelsea Drainage Department' and up the stairs to the room where our wedding was taking place.

Tim looked very glamorous, but the short ceremony turned out to be a bit of an ordeal for all concerned, as the registrar seemed to have a weird speech impediment which only started when he began the official proceedings. I spent ten minutes not daring to look at anyone, desperately trying not to laugh. Outside, we posed for photos, and then it was off to Soho for lunch. My sister announced that she was giving me an ironing board –

she'd been smoking frantically in order to accumulate enough cigarette coupons to get it for free.

Apart from the fact that Tim's granny (a tiny little Yorkshire woman known to the family as Goggie) got herself locked in the men's toilet and had to be released by Mario, the Terrazza's owner, the lunch passed off without incident. My mother drank a bit too much and slightly disgraced herself by deciding to take home the flowers that decorated the table ('I've paid for the bloody things, so I'm bloody well taking them'). The roses were actually wired into their vases, so Mario soon stepped in and diplomatically gave her the container as well. Soon, Marjorie and Goggie were also clutching vases full of wedding flowers, and were weaving their way back across Dean Street to the car park. Tim and I hailed a taxi, loaded it with presents (thankfully, the ironing board hadn't arrived) and headed back to Chelsea to get ready for our party.

On arrival at Hereford House we encountered a problem – my new husband had forgotten the keys to our flat, and George was nowhere to be found. Luckily, the block was being repainted, and scaffolding covered the front, all the way up to the roof guttering. Our flat, No 22, was on the fourth floor, and Tim gingerly made his way up through the scaffolding poles and planking. I couldn't look – we'd only been married four hours and I couldn't bear the idea that he might fall! He managed to pull down the living-room window and open the door. We couldn't wait to get our wedding clothes off and make love, then have a bath, then push our few bits of furniture to the walls, put out the glasses, uncork the wine and stick out some crisps, sausage rolls, sandwiches and snacks. I changed into a little romper suit of blue velvet, designed by my friend Paul Babb for Twiggy's clothing range, much more sexy and fun than Ossie's limp frock.

The party was brilliant – people brought us some wonderful presents, and everyone seemed to have a good time. Joe Tilson generously stumped up a pair of his latest silkscreen prints, of New York skyscrapers, shaped like large Decals. Other people gave us old magazines, bits of art deco, and a funny old Harrison Marks fifties movie of nude girls for our slide-show evenings. Quite a few people gave us small amounts of drugs – a couple of tabs of LSD, half a dozen spliffs and a couple of tablets that could have been speed. We danced till four in the morning to Nico and the Velvet Underground, and, when all the

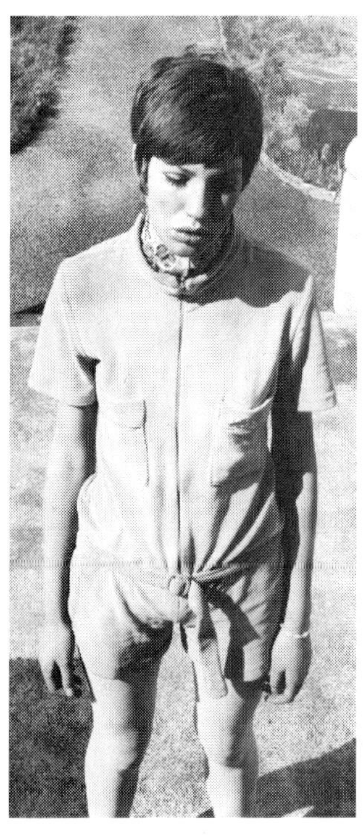

guests had gone, fell asleep on our mattress in the living room. Tim had built a platform so we could lie in bed and look out over the rooftops of Chelsea. I put a pillow over my head to block out the impending daylight and snuggled under my home-made patchwork quilt.

We drove down to Cornwall the next day and stayed in the large stone guest cottage (known as The Poor House!) next to Patrick Heron's house, enjoying evenings listening to the wind whistle outside, watching pine cones burn on the fire in the grate, eating crayfish and gurnard, bought from Newlyn fish market, on the pine kitchen table. Days were spent walking over the moors down to the cliffs at Pendeen and Treen and along by the sea, investigating rock pools and picking up round stones eroded by the waves to decorate our bathroom in London. It was cold, but there were no tourists, and the light was dazzling. We went for lunch with Patrick and his wife, Delia, next door, sitting in their spacious kitchen eating home-made brown bread, drinking white wine and enjoying all his slanderous gossip about the London art scene. Patrick was an excellent mimic, and there was no one he could not parody to perfection.

After six days of rest and isolation, we decided to stop

off in Bristol on our way back to London, to see Tim's sister Rosalind, who was at University there, and go to a party on the Saturday night.

When we arrived at our friends' house in Clifton, they were hysterical: 'You've got to drive straight back to London. George has been on the telephone – the police have broken down your front door and taken loads of stuff from the flat.'

We rang George at once. It was all true. The previous night he'd got home from work to find the door hanging off its hinges, and a note telling him to call the local police station, where we were requested to attend for an interview. I started crying; I was completely terrified.

One of the people at the party had the good idea of telephoning a drugs helpline in London – they used to advertise regularly in underground magazines, because the police were starting to pursue cannabis users really aggressively. We told the woman who took our call what had happened, and she was immediately calming and sympathetic and said on no account should we go back to the flat without a lawyer. She told us to ring again in the morning, by which time she would have fixed one up for us. I couldn't enjoy the party after that. We begged George not to leave the flat, otherwise stuff would get stolen. Tim told him to patch up the front door by nailing up some wood across the inside so he could at least get a night's sleep.

We crashed with friends, but I spent a sleepless night. Why on earth had the police picked on us? The papers were full of all the drug raids on famous pop stars like the Stones, but we were nobodies, even if we did live in Chelsea near the Kings Road. The only things I could think of were the envelope marked 'DRUGS!' and the fact that we'd talked about putting hash in the wedding cake. But the amount of stuff in the flat was negligible, really. Although we were friends with some of the people who worked on the underground magazine *Oz* (Felix Dennis often used to come round to our flat after work), Tim and I had never said anything publicly about drugs, and neither of us had bothered to attend the Legalize Pot rally in Hyde Park earlier in the summer – it just wasn't that central to our lives.

We drove up to London the next day and met the lawyer at a café. He told us we would go to the police station together, but that he had to do all the talking.

Once in the building, we identified ourselves and were shown to an interview room. A detective entered the room with a large package. Out of it he took the two envelopes marked 'DRUGS!' and 'PORN!' and placed them on the table in front of us. He then unwrapped my cake tin, and opened it to reveal the bottom layer of my wedding cake. He leaned over the table and asked, 'Mr and Mrs Street-Porter, do these items belong to you?' Whereupon our solicitor said, 'My clients will not be answering your questions. I would like to ask you if you were in possession of a search warrant when you entered 22 Hereford House last Friday and broke the lock on the front door when you could not get an answer to the doorbell.'

There was a silence that seemed interminable, while the two men stared at each other. I was trembling, locking my hands under my knees so they couldn't see how scared I was. 'The interview is terminated,' said the detective. 'Will you please wait outside?'

After about fifteen minutes the lawyer appeared in the corridor. 'You can go now,' he said. 'You're bloody lucky. They didn't have a search warrant, they were just chancing their luck. They won't be pressing charges.' I was momentarily speechless, and then plucked up the courage to ask: 'Do you think I could have my wedding cake back, please?'

We had to wait two weeks, while the police sent the cake to the laboratory for forensic testing, in case they could find traces of narcotics. Of course, there were none, but when I'd collected it from the nick and signed a chit to say I'd received it in good condition, I opened the tin and found that holes had been drilled through it in every direction. It looked more like a bit of Gruyere than a fruit cake. I had to cut round the cavities when I finally sent the little pieces of cake out to the relatives, packed in silver and white boxes. Mum kept moaning about why I was taking so long – if only she'd known!

Of course, I realised months later that the police were absolutely furious that they'd been outmanoeuvred. After all, it's not every day you go on a drugs raid and come across an envelope with 'DRUGS!' written on it. We were very careful after that, and if George and Tim wanted to smoke dope they didn't do it at home. We continued as before, hanging out with the girls in the flat upstairs – Diana (Diney) Biurski, who was at the LSE, a student activist and anti-war pacifist, and her friend Katie (who had found us George to help pay our rent), who was a teacher.

On Sunday, 17 March 1968, we all went on the first anti-Vietnam-war demonstration, marching through London to Trafalgar Square for speeches and then on to the American Embassy in Grosvenor Square. There were about fifty thousand people chanting and singing on that march, from ordinary students and young men and women to celebrities – the rage at the American government was enormous. It felt like a historic moment, certainly the largest demonstration I had ever seen.

When we got to Grosvenor Square and the US Embassy, things started to turn nasty. We chucked plastic bags filled with blood (which we'd got from the butcher's near us in Chelsea) at the police – other people threw missiles, too – and the people at the front of the march rolled marbles under the hooves of the police horses as they charged towards us. I turned and there was Mick Jagger, legging it over a hedge. By the time the police charged the crowd a second time, with truncheons flailing, Tim and I decided it was too scary and we, too, ran for our lives down South Audley Street towards the bottom of Park Lane and the undergound station at Hyde Park Corner. Next day in the paper it said that 117 police had been injured and hundreds of people had been arrested.

All over Europe young people were taking to the streets and expressing their displeasure with those in control. Martin Luther King was murdered on 4 April. Then there were student riots in Poland and in Berlin. On 21 April Enoch Powell made his inflammatory 'rivers of blood' speech about the numbers of immigrants arriving in Britain. Students occupied Hornsey and Guilford art schools. In June Robert Kennedy was assassinated. Now there were student riots in Berkeley, Tim's old stamping ground, and in August the Biafran war began, and Russian tanks rolled into Czechoslovakia. It was a momentous time.

In Hereford House we chilled out by listening to Van Morrison's trippy *Astral Weeks*, and went with the girls upstairs and George to the Palm House in Kew Gardens, where Tim photographed us all frolicking with huge branches outside the beautiful curved glass of the Victorian hothouse. Another outing took us to Clevedon Pier outside Bristol, where Diney wore one of the silver coats I made for boutiques in Carnaby Street, and posed on the deck chairs. We partied a lot in London, hanging out in pubs off Portobello Road and Notting Hill Gate with artists who'd just left Chelsea and St Martin's. I'd just started my job as home editor of *Petticoat* (a weekly magazine for young women) and was having a whale of a time, organising photo shoots and commissioning illustrations for my pages.

Meanwhile, our friend Molly Parkin, who was fashion editor of the innovative *Nova* magazine, had got involved with a very weird fellow called Hector Binney, who she'd met at the Chelsea Arts Club in Old Church Street when she lived in a house just down the street. The besotted

man used to come up to town and ferry her around London in his ancient Bentley.

Molly had a reputation for consuming vast quantities of booze and for outrageous behaviour, but even she seemed to have met her match with Hector. He was in his fifties, the son of a famous admiral. He seemed to be the black sheep of the family, and had no real job, as far as I could make out. His family seat was Pampisford Hall, a crumbling Victorian mansion in parkland about ten miles from Cambridge. Tim and I were invited down there for the weekend, along with our friends Peter and Jane Murray. Peter had been at college with me and Jane worked as a fashion writer with Molly on *Nova*.

When we arrived on the Friday evening, a long driveway flanked with tall gloomy conifers took us up to the main entrance of a Palladian villa with crumbling columns. I felt as if we were taking part in a Hammer Horror production – the feeling of dread was definitely enhanced by the depth of the shade in the woodland on every side: Hector proudly informed me that the estate contained one of the largest collections of evergreens in the country.

Our host's mood was initially perky, and he set Jane and me to work to prepare dinner, while we waited for Molly to arrive. Tim and Peter tried as best they could to entertain him. Although the place was vast, we could see no staff. I wandered upstairs and chose a bedroom, finding some sheets in a linen cupboard.

Downstairs, the kitchen was completely filthy and Hector's idea of shopping seemed to be a couple of chickens, frozen peas and some bags of potatoes. The fridge was full of mysterious rotting leftovers, and cats wandered in and out. We peeled the spuds – enough for twelve – and put the chickens to roast in the oven. In the dining room the long mahogany table would have easily accommodated twenty. I found some linen napkins and place mats, and Hector insisted we used the very best silver, unlocking a series of strongrooms full of tureens, candlesticks, cutlery and serving dishes. The wine cellar yielded dusty bottles of excellent claret. By the time Jane and I had finished our preparations the table looked fit for a monarch, let alone Molly Parkin.

By eight thirty there was still no sign of Molly, and Hector was getting distinctly tetchy – this was before the age of the mobile phone so he had no way of knowing if she was en route, or even coming at all, as there was no answer from her Chelsea home. We were all getting decidedly drunk, and decided to serve dinner, carving the chickens and filling the tureens with roast potatoes and frozen peas – what a feast! It was a sweltering evening and we kept the French doors open onto the garden throughout the meal. Most of the other guests were our friends from student days; Hector hardly knew them.

When we'd finished, he demanded we played strip poker, dealing out the cards on top of the wine-stained linen tablecloth, and quickly engineered a situation whereby he was down to his underpants. Jane and I were smart enough at cards (and sufficiently level-headed) to keep most of our clothes on, which enraged Hector no end. After about thirty minutes he started bellowing with rage, and stormed out of the room, returning with a large whip in one hand, waving it about in frenzied fashion, screaming orders to 'Get your kit off!' We quickly ran though the French doors onto the moonlit lawn, which now seemed welcoming and not the slightest bit gloomy. Bats flitted in and out of the trees and we could hear an owl. We crept round to the other side of the house, let ourselves in through a back door, and quietly shuffled up the stairs to bed, leaving Hector slumped in the drawing room with the whip and the port decanter.

Next morning Molly still had not arrived, and there was no mention of Hector's little 'turn' the night before when he eventually surfaced for breakfast. After a walk with him to the village pub for lunch, Tim and I said our goodbyes, got into the Porsche and drove back to London, and sanity. Molly subsequently claimed she had 'told the old fart I wasn't coming down anyway', and roared with laughter when she heard about the strip poker and the whip. Hector soon bit the dust.

Throughout the spring of 1968 Tim and I gradually forgot about that horrible night in Bristol and the ensuing contretemps with the drugs squad. The front door to our flat was mended, I learned to cook a bit (more than fruit cakes and chicken, anyway!), and we installed in the living room a cardboard table and chairs left over from my 'D is for Disposable' spread in the 'A to Z of Live-In' I was writing for *Petticoat*. But the police had not forgotten about us. They were determined to settle unfinished business.

It was about seven o'clock on a beautiful summer's

evening and I'd just returned from work. It was hot, and I opened the kitchen window and was thinking of taking a lukewarm bath before we went out to a party later. Tim was in the office, looking through contact sheets. George was lying on the bed in his room, smoking and taking potshots with an air rifle at an Airfix model plane suspended by thread from the ceiling. The crisp thwack of the pellets hitting the wall cut through the sounds of Pink Floyd coming from the stereo in the living room. Suddenly, there was heavy banging on the front door, and a man's voice shouted, 'Open up!' As I drew back the door, a group of policemen in uniform barged past me, with a couple of men in suits who flashed bits of card at me at me, shouting, 'Step aside, please! Police! We have warrants.'

I was terrified – I couldn't believe we were being raided again – what on earth would happen this time? Tim, George and I were herded into the living room, where a policeman in uniform told us to sit down and wait. We could hear the sounds of our flat being ripped apart further down the corridor. In the office, files were taken out of the cabinet and turned upside down, books were pulled from shelves higgledy-piggledy, and papers, bills, photographs, newspaper cuttings and letters fell everywhere. Further down the hall, all our clothes were taken out of the wardrobe and chucked on the floor, the chest of drawers emptied in a heap. We sat in the front room on the edge of the raised wooden sleeping platform Tim had built, watched by a uniformed policeman.

Suddenly, one of the squad burst into the room and with a flourish produced a tiny piece of hash – the size of small fingernail – holding it in front of me. 'I found this in your wardrobe,' he announced to Tim and me. 'I'm afraid you'll have to come down to the station, and' – pausing for full effect, he produced an ancient silver bullet – 'I am afraid,' he continued, looking at George, 'that this was found in your bedside cupboard, and you will have to come as well.' The three of us were open-mouthed. Since the raid nine months earlier, we'd been extremely careful not to have any drugs at all at home – it just wasn't worth the risk. I had no idea how it had got there, but there was absolutely nothing we could do about it; it was going to be their word against ours. As for the bullet, without a gun it was hardly a lethal weapon.

Next, we had to hand over the keys to our clapped-out

old Mini, and then the three of us filed down the stairs of Hereford House and into a police van parked outside. One of the officers picked up our car from a side street just round the corner and drove towards the nick. At the police station we were separated, and I was locked in a cell for a couple of hours, not allowed to use the telephone or speak to anyone. I screamed the place down and kicked the door constantly. Eventually, around 10 p.m., I was fingerprinted against my will – two men holding my arms down – and told I would be charged with possessing dangerous drugs. Would I like to make a statement? Of course not. I was saying absolutely nothing. 'We'll take that as a denial, then,' the man on the other side of the desk in the windowless interview room told me. I ignored him. Tim was going through the same process in another room. George was also fingerprinted, and charged with possessing an offensive weapon.

When we all met on the pavement outside, I was literally shaking with rage. How dare those bastards do this! I didn't even smoke pot, and certainly didn't keep it at home. How fucking pathetic of these strutting, macho tossers! We were not allowed to drive our car back home as the fuzz were busy stripping it down to 'search' for more drugs. We went to a call box down the street and called the Release emergency number (a help switchboard), desperate to tell someone sympathetic our story. We were busted, caught up in it right up to our armpits, exactly as had already happened to the well-known modern-art dealer Robert Fraser, and of course the Rolling Stones – Mick Jagger, Brian Jones and Keith Richards.

In the following days, it seemed to me and a lot of other people I talked to that some police officers were hell bent on achieving fame and a high media profile with the number of well-known people they managed to catch with LSD or cannabis. But why us? We weren't well known, just an architectural photographer, a young writer on a teenage magazine and a Latin teacher – all of us at the start of our careers.

I had just started my first job as a journalist and I didn't want to mess it up. So this time, I had to make a tough decision. Tim and I talked to the solicitor we'd consulted before, and he told us there was no point in pleading not guilty, because if we did the case would go to a jury and there would be maximum publicity. Best to grit our teeth, plead guilty, and hope that no one noticed.

A couple of weeks later we turned up at Great Marlborough Street magistrates court on the appointed day. I'd told the *Petticoat* office I had a dentist appointment, and wore the longest skirt I could find, no make-up, and a plain jumper. Tim wore his wedding suit and a tie. His long hair was combed behind his ears; there was nothing he could do about the moustache. We were kept waiting for an hour or so while dozens of cases were heard, and then finally we were called. In the dock the charges were read, one by one; I was perspiring a bit with nerves, clenching my fists tightly. Tim and I said, 'Guilty,' when asked how we would plead. The magistrate didn't even look at us, banged his gavel and said, 'Fined five pounds.' George received a £5 fine for possessing the silver bullet. How bloody ridiculous! The whole event was over in less than five minutes, less time than it had taken us to get married. We went to the pub for a drink, but I didn't feel like celebrating. Thankfully, there was no mention of the proceedings in any of the papers the next day. We'd had a lucky escape – I wouldn't be making another mistake like that again. I couldn't be anywhere near policemen for about five years after that second raid – they made my flesh creep, even though my own uncle was a long-serving copper in the Fulham police force throughout the whole period. He has long since retired, having spent the last part of his career doing nothing more aggressive than running the car pound where motorists had to pay stiff fines to retrieve their illegally parked vehicles.

After the court case things never seemed the same at

22 Hereford House. Tim and I decided that we could manage the rent now that I was working full-time, so George said goodbye. He'd found a nice girlfriend, and we hoped he'd be able to live with her. George was a bit lost. He was fed up with teaching Latin at a school where no one was interested, but didn't know what to do instead, unlike Tim and me, who were super-focused on our careers. George was highly intelligent, but in danger of going nowhere.

We decorated the bedroom dark brown, painting over the wall which George had hit when firing his air-gun at model planes. We installed a large brass bed and dismantled the sleeping platform in the front room, replacing it with an art deco three-piece suite we'd bought down the road in Fulham Broadway and had reupholstered in pink velvet fabric from Biba.

George went travelling, and we didn't hear anything about him for a couple of years. Then a girl I met in the street in Soho one day told me he'd been busted in Rome and was serving a three-year sentence in appalling conditions in prison there. I never saw him again, and heard rumours that he was dead.

Chapter 2

Between the first and second drug busts, I had started my new career as a full-time journalist. By the end of my second year at the Architectural Association I had gradually stopped going into college, and had decided to take a year off. I'd applied to continue my studies at Columbia University in New York, and it would take another year to get any kind of bursary. After the summer holidays I wrote some sample articles about design and mailed them off to a handful of magazine editors in the hope of landing a lowly job in journalism.

I was very excited when Audrey Slaughter, editor of *Honey* magazine (a monthly for young women), called me up to her offices just off Fleet Street and after a short interview offered me a job on a new magazine called

Petticoat, which was to be launched in February 1968. I was given the grand title of home editor and would be in charge of several pages in each issue, writing articles about interiors and commissioning photographs. All for the sum of £18.50 a week!

For the first time there was to be a weekly magazine aimed at young women my age. It was an exciting prospect, working with a group of young women like Frankie McGowan (whose sister Cathy had presented *Ready Steady Go*) and Lauren Wade. Lynne Franks was our secretary! I had to write a spread a week, commission the photographers and illustrators to work with me, come up with ideas for features about design and fashion. Soon I was working with people like Michael Roberts (who had just left High Wycombe art school), Terry Gillian (who came to live in London and had drawn a strip for *Playboy* in the US) and the graphic designer Philip Castle.

Among the designers whose work I featured was Zandra Rhodes; she and her long-suffering boyfriend and business partner, Alex McIntyre, became very close friends of Tim and me. I'd first encountered them while I was still at the Architectural Association and they were in their final year at the Royal College of Art. My college pal Peter Murray and I went to a party in Paddington and were entranced by this stylish couple who looked quite unlike anyone else. Zandra's hair was short and bobbed, dyed navy blue. She had painted black and white checks from her eyelids up to her eyebrows. Alex was very glamorous, with the longest hair I'd seen on a man. They seemed a formidable pair, and I was too shy to say hello to these style icons.

Zandra's mother had worked for a Parisian couturier, and her father had been a lorry driver from Chatham. Alex came from a working-class family who lived in a terraced house in Oldham, a bleak suburb of Manchester, where he'd gone to art school before the Royal College.

When we met again in 1968, Zandra was in partner-

ship with Sylvia Ayton, working out of a tiny upstairs office on the corner of Shaftesbury Avenue and Monmouth Street in the West End. Soon they began cutting patterns and fitting clothes on me, because I was a perfect size ten and looked great in their designs. In those days Sylvia was the dressmaker and Zandra the fabric designer, but that was soon to change. They had an extremely fractious relationship, to put it mildly. Over the years I came to believe that Zandra, a bit like me, has only one of doing things, her way, and there is no point in trying to reason with her or instil any ideas of partnership: she's on another waveband, on planet Zandra. That's what makes her unique – and also impossible.

Her prints were a novel take on pop art – lines of electric light bulbs, cartoon cutout little men, fluorescent swirls, and, of course, lipsticks. Barbara Huluaniki was at the height of her success, with her Biba Store in Kensington Church Street so popular that she decided to expand and open a department store in the old art deco Derry and Toms building around the corner on Kensington High Street. The Biba style was clinging, vampish, with art deco inspired prints on velvet and jersey. Zandra used canvas, cotton and even paper for some disposable wedding dresses, which she sold in packets. Ossie Clark's style was bias cut, beautifully shaped and sexy, with Celia Birtwell's soft prints on black crepe and cream silk chiffon – very floaty and feminine. I was friendly with Ossie and Barbara, and wore their clothes, but Zandra was always a loner, both socially and in her designs. She was never interested in being acceptable, part of a group. She had the sheer bloody single-mindedness to stick to what she thought was right, even when it proved hard to sell.

Zandra and Sylvia opened their Fulham Road shop in

1967 with a tremendous party, at which Joe Cocker sang (he had a huge hit at the time, 'With a Little Help from My Friends') – a complete knockout! Of course it proved very hard to keep the shop going after that initial

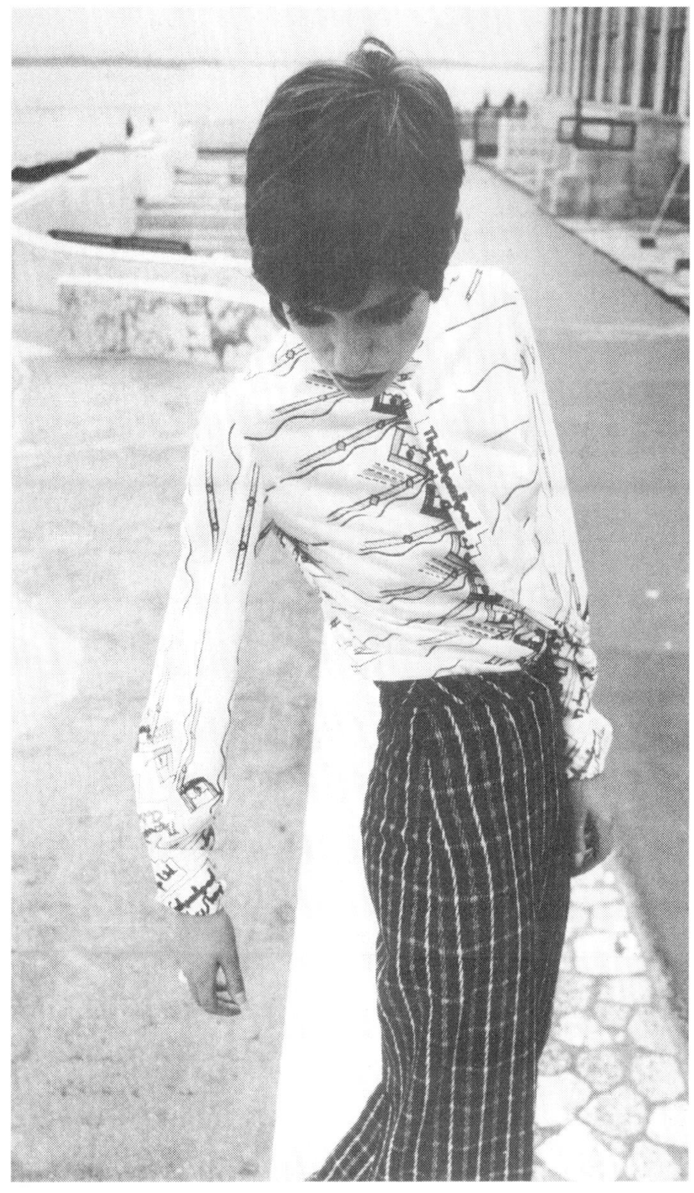

crowded launch. There weren't too many people willing to wear cream silk tea dresses printed with lipsticks or canvas coats with lightbulbs on them, but Zandra persevered.

Tim and I were huge fans, and I decided to help out by photographing some of the clothes for *Petticoat*. I modelled the clothes as part of a session shot outside the art deco Hoover factory on the A40 in west London (just down the road from my parents' house in Perivale) and at Jaywick Sands outside Clacton. I wore a floor-length PVC raincoat with fake python inserts on the shoulders by Zandra and Sylvia, as well as a striking black and red tweed trouser suit. I sported emerald-green suede knee-length boots with long ties, from the Chelsea Cobbler. The cover picture showed me in a red jersey coat with a long printed scarf by Zandra. Tim went round to their silkscreen workshop on Porchester Road in Notting Hill Gate and photographed Alex painstakingly printing their designs, with a bandana made from an old T-shirt tied round his shoulder-length hair.

In 1969 Yves St Laurent came to London and opened the first Rive Gauche boutique on Bond Street, a seminal moment for couture, marking the start of their diffusion of cheaper lines. At the launch party I wore a long jersey cardigan coat printed with a wild landscape made of knitting, designed by Zandra. Although his English was limited, I was thrilled that Yves stopped and talked to me about my outfit, telling me he 'adored' Zandra's designs.

But not even his adoration could save her shop. Eventually, it had to close and Zandra and Sylvia went their separate ways. Zandra was later to stage a fashion show at the Round House and get adopted by Beatrix Miller at British *Vogue* – a critical piece of patronage because it led to press coverage in America and sales to the Henri Bendel store in New York. She started to build up a very varied range of wealthy customers, from Drue Heinz to Diana Ross and the actress Irene Worth.

All through the summer of 1969 I carried a red plastic typewriter everywhere we went – to the countryside in Dorset and Somerset, up to the Cheviots in Northumberland. In Milan Tim had met a charismatic man called Ettore Sottsass, one of the chief designers for Olivetti. But Sottsass was more than a product designer. He'd studied architecture in Turin in the 1930s, and after the Second World War had set up an office in Milan, designing everything from buildings to furniture and china and gadgets. He was interested in the East, in mysticism, and on one of his trips to London met a bunch of people who were followers of an Indian mystic called Meher Baba. (The previous year the Beatles had spent eleven weeks in India, meditating with the Mahesh Yogi Maharishi.) Sottsass was amazingly curious about all sorts of things – he'd started a literary magazine with the American poet Allen Ginsburg in 1967, and the following year was awarded an honorary degree by the Royal College of Art in London. He loved the city, and often stopped off for a day or so on his way to or from America.

Tim was soon photographing buildings and projects for Sottsass in Milan and was thrilled to be asked to contribute to the advertising campaign for a brand-new product Sottsass was launching for Olivetti. The Valentine typewriter looked completely different from any bit of office equipment you'd seen before. The body and carrying case were made of moulded bright red plastic – it was light, portable and completely desirable. The case snapped shut with two pieces of black rubber. At a time when many designers were influenced by art deco and

the 1930s, or the swirling plant forms of art nouveau, Sottsass was a true revolutionary, only interested in the present, an intellectual, obsessed with making design accessible and fun for the mass market. Instead of creating an advertising campaign which placed his product in glamorous settings, he asked photographers, film-makers and graphic designers whose work he admired in many different countries to photograph, film or draw it being used and carried by their friends and people they came into contact with. It was a ground-breaking way of launching a new product.

Through Ettore we met a graphic designer called Mike McInnery, who had designed the unforgettably surreal artwork for the album of the Who's rock opera, *Tommy*, released the previous year. Mike had also been asked to work on the Valentine campaign. He lived with his wife, Kate, on the ground floor of an Edwardian mansion (once the home of the actress Lily Langtry) surrounded by a shady garden, near the Thames just outside Richmond, and soon we would head over there for parties or musical evenings in the warm summer months, driving in our old Mini.

It was funny we hadn't met Mike before, because our paths had taken a similar course in many ways. In 1966 we'd all frequented the short-lived underground UFO club, off Tottenham Court Road, where musicians like Arthur Brown, Jimi Hendrix, Pink Floyd and Procol Harum performed, and Mike had painted murals while Tim had shown his slides. Like us, Mike had also produced posters (we'd designed some using images of futuristic space craft and imaginary cities, culled from old comics, for a pop promoter, but he reneged on the deal and we nearly lost a lot of money when he cancelled the print run at short notice).

This was a time when places like Kensington Market were full of stalls selling posters, designed by people like Nigel Weymouth and Martin Sharp, of pop stars like Hendrix and the Rolling Stones. In America, a new wave of graphic design – seen in the psychedelic posters for the Avalon Ballroom outside San Francisco and the extraordinary comics produced by people like Robert Crumb (with names like *Sweet Annie Fanny* and *The Furry Freak Brothers*) – was already highly collectable. Now, in the aftermath of flower power, posters, small privately printed comics and magazines were all being snapped up by collectors, and young people wanted them to put on their bedroom walls.

Mike had studied at the London College of Printing in 1964, but dropped out and soon got work decorating tea shops and coffee bars with his murals, and he'd been art director of an underground newspaper, the *International Times*. He'd also done work for Felix Dennis, Martin

Sharp and Richard Neville's subversive magazine *Oz*, which had started in January 1967.

When the Obscene Publications Squad (attached to Holborn police) raided *IT* later that year and closed it down, we all attended the fund-raising event at Alexandra Palace in north London, the Fourteen-Hour Technicolour Dream, the first all-night rave (Tim and I got completely stoned during the proceedings). Just inside the entrance to the building a funfair had been erected, complete with a helter-skelter, which became more and more unruly as the evening went on. There were art events and 'happenings', including one in which you were invited to cut the clothes off Yoko Ono – most people were too embarrassed to participate. We wandered through the vast space in a complete haze, drinking in the heady atmosphere. As the dawn rose and Pink Floyd were playing, I became aware of a man perched precariously on a parapet high above the crowd. Soon we were all shouting 'Jump! Jump! Jump!' He'd clearly taken acid and was frozen, unable to decide what to do. Security guards moved in, a ladder was found, and he was bundled away, much to everyone's disappointment. Mike was there, but our paths didn't cross.

Like us, he'd moved on from the underground scene, and just as I now had a job on the *Daily Mail*, and Tim was making a name for himself as a photographer for the glossy magazines, Mike worked as a freelance illustrator for the *Sunday Times* and *Nova* magazine, as well as *Reader's Digest* in America. His work was always mystical and dreamlike, heavily influenced by the teachings of the Indian mystic Meher Baba. Baba's philosophy could be summed up simply as 'Be happy' or 'Love Baba and your troubles will be worthwhile but they won't be over.' From 1925 until his death (in 1969) Meher Baba didn't speak, communicating by hand gestures which were interpreted by his disciples. As to why, he sent his followers this message: 'To get nearer and nearer to God you have to get further and further away from "I, my, me, mine". You have not to renounce anything but your own self. It is as simple as that, though found to be almost impossible.' Baba claimed to be the Avatar, a Sanskrit word meaning 'descended from God', an ancient soul who is God in human form.

In 1967 Mike McInnery had got talking to an actress in her seventies called Delia de Leon at a poetry society meeting – she had met Meher Baba on his first trip in

England in the 1930s, and had been a follower ever since. Delia was a grey-haired, elegant woman who couldn't fail to impress you with her air of calm and spirituality. Mike had been living in Shaftesbury Avenue, but moved down to Twickenham, just over the river from Richmond, to be nearer Delia, who lived in Kew and was the undisputed focus of the Meher Baba movement in England. Mike enthused about the Baba philosophy to Pete Townshend, with whom he was working very closely during the recording of the Who's huge *Tommy* project, the story of a boy who could not see, hear or feel anything, told through a series of pop songs. It was to be hailed as the first 'rock opera' by the critics, who praised its bold vision and abundance of catchy tunes.

Pete and Mike had first met at UFO and Karen, Pete's wife, designed clothes for Mike's wedding in 1967. Karen's flat in Victoria soon became the Baba centre in the UK, financed by a committee who kept the library full and organised meetings. After a while Pete and Karen moved down to Twickenham, too, buying a beautiful Georgian house which overlooked the river, and the Baba centre moved nearby. Pete and Mike were the closest of mates, and through our friendship with Mike we soon knew Pete and Karen, too. I always found it extraordinary that on stage Pete would smash up his guitars – his favourite tutor at art school had been the auto-destructive artist Gustav Metzger, who had staged some pieces at the Architectural Association when I was studying there, one of which involved destroying a piano. I couldn't quite reconcile the brilliant theatricality of Pete's stage version of this, performing anthemic pop classics like 'Hope I Die Before I Get Too Old' or 'My Generation', with Baba's calm and cerebral view of the world. But Pete was a huge Baba fan, and so were Ronnie Lane of the Small Faces and his wife, Sue, who were also regulars round at the McInnerys', where we'd sit under the trees, listen to music, drink wine, and some people would smoke dope.

Pete Townshend was a well-known musician, but he was struggling to reconcile his spiritual life with the demands of stardom, and all its excesses. The Who were famous for the sheer energy, noise and exuberance of their performances – live at places like the Marquee, they absolutely took your breath away. But when you met him in a small group, as at Mike's, Pete was thoughtful, highly intelligent, somewhat secretive and private; he told *Rolling Stone* in an interview published in November 1970: 'I never met Baba, never wrote him a letter or received one . . . I'm not hanging on, I'm stuck on. People could easily get the idea that I'm an unwilling Baba lover or "Baba tryer" as I prefer to call myself . . . Baba helps, is doing things for you and your life that you will never perceive. Here am I, in suburban Twickenham, skinny, vain, and obsessed with the word "forward": how am I equipped to begin to understand eternal love?'

Throughout the summer of 1969 Tim must have photographed the Valentine typewriter in hundreds of locations, sending all the transparencies off to Ettore in Milan, who declared himself thril-led with the result. He gave us the typewriter and a red plastic cut out of it which had been used for advert-ising displays. We hung it on the wall of our flat, like an artwork.

Mike and Kate still came over and visited us, but we were never going to sign up to all that Meher Baba stuff, so our friendship was never going to progress beyond a certain point. Then Kate ran off with Ronnie Lane, leaving Sue, his wife, and Mike, devastated. As their tightly-knit group disintegrated, Mike and I gradually went our separate ways.

Tim and I stood on the rocky headland in the blazing midday sun and tried to make the poles and canvas he'd unpacked from a kitbag turn into a tent. The trip hadn't started well – we'd flown into Palma airport on a cheap flight and arrived late at night with nowhere to stay in Majorca. The plan was to have a cheap summer break camping on a piece of land on the neighbouring island of Formentera owned by my friend from college, Peter Murray. The only time I'd ever camped before was a couple of nights as a Girl Guide, when my troop had been taken to Epping Forest. I had not enjoyed it – the weather was freezing and damp, and all we had to eat was beans and burnt sausages. At least the Mediterranean in August was baking hot.

Formentera had a reputation as a hippy hangout, less developed than Majorca, with just one tarmac road and an unmarked network of dirt tracks. There were a few villas owned by Germans along one sandy beach, and a couple of hotels and a café. People would come for lunch by boat and then leave in the late afternoon – there were few rooms to be had. We'd spent the previous night huddled together on the quayside in Palma, sheltering between two large wooden crates, trying to doze, wrapped in blankets because we couldn't find a cheap hotel room and the ferry left at 6 a.m. anyway.

Now, befuddled from lack of sleep, I was rapidly losing my patience with Tim. It turned out that he'd managed to hire a tent for a single small person, with poles from a different-sized one. Eventually we got it assembled, but it would only hold me. Tim would have to sleep on a groundsheet next to it in a sleeping bag. So much for a romantic start!

We stowed our rucksacks and kitbags in the tent, zipped it up and, making sure we had our money and cameras, trudged off through the scrub and down to the beach, heading for the café and some lunch. It was full of long-haired American men and women, whose only conversation seemed to be 'Wow!' or 'Neat!' The private houses were surrounded by barbed wire with 'KEEP OUT' and 'PRIVATE' notices every ten yards. There was obviously a turf war going on between the summer dropouts and the wealthy homeowners.

But Formentera was beautiful, if basic, with a rocky hillock at one end (where we'd attempted to set up camp), which culminated in a lighthouse. At the other end was a long finger of flat land stretching towards Majorca, which was covered in salt flats, their shimmering whiteness adding to the feeling of unreality about the place. The long, narrow central section of the island had a sandy beach on either side.

That night I didn't sleep a wink. We'd hung out in the beach bar after supper, listening to hippies playing the guitar and enthusing about the sunset – 'Wow, that was really neat!' – and then made our way up the hill in the moonlight, cursing ourselves for not bringing a torch. We stumbled through some very thorny bushes, and I moaned as my legs got scratched. Finally, we found our little tent, and after I'd had a pee in the bushes we rolled out the groundsheet and sleeping bag for Tim. I curled up inside the tent – I zipped it up to keep out bugs but it was boiling hot, so I opened the flaps and lay on top of my sleeping bag, desperate for some sleep. I eventually dozed off, but I was woken up by the sound of rustling in the bushes. I sat up and grabbed my glasses just in time to see a rat the size of a small cat saunter through our clearing. That was it. I woke Tim and made him cram himself into the tent with me, dozing fitfully until dawn.

We packed up the tent and walked in silence back down to the road. There was no way I was spending a moment longer surrounded by rodents. Exhausted, I dragged myself back along the beach to the sand outside the only hotel. The moment we saw signs of life we went in and ordered coffee and bread, and I attempted to wash in the toilets. At reception I asked if there were any rooms. The man behind the desk just laughed – it was August, the height of the season, and they had been fully booked for months. I was desperate, and begged him for a room of any description. We had almost two weeks until our return flight from Majorca – what were we to do? I asked him to take my name and put us on a waiting list; we'd be back to ask every day. For two nights we slept on the beach in front of the hotel, a discreet distance away, and I used the toilets as my bathroom.

I had a very trendy wardrobe for someone camping – after all I was writing about fashion, and had blagged loads of free clothes to wear on my holiday. At Zandra's Fulham Clothes Shop, I had purchased a pair of white cotton shorts printed with blue, red and lipsticks for a bargain price of just £3. They had a red waistband which tied in a big bow at the back, just the thing when you're sleeping rough and washing in a public lavatory! I wore them for one of my begging trips to the hotel reception, and they must have brought me luck, because we were told there was a room we could have for the next week and a bit. I paid a deposit, and sauntered back to tell Tim the good news.

1	Pair Lipstick Cotton Shorts	3	3	–
	Great Summer Reduction for advertising on Formenterra.			
	£	3	3	–

000165

The room turned out to be in the basement, and virtually windowless with just a small shutter opening onto a wall, but we didn't care. Anything was better than camping! Our new home had no ventilation except for the door, so it was absolutely boiling, but at least we had a bed and a shower. We scored some LSD off the hippies on the beach and took it one morning when we'd walked out to the salt flats. I was slightly nervous because we'd heard local gossip about a young man who had jumped to his death off the cliffs near the lighthouse on a bad acid trip the previous month. In the event, very little happened. I walked around slowly and aimlessly in circles, and a spider's web on a bush captured my attention for hours; it seemed to get larger and smaller as I watched it, totally fixated on the intricacy of the web. The dazzling white of the saltflats made my eyes ache – I was probably staring at the sun for too long without realising it. The bleached dunes pulsated and throbbed in the heat. When the sun was sinking into the sea, we pulled ourselves up from the bank we'd been stretched out on, and slowly walked back to the hotel. I

was exhausted – the trip must have lasted about seven or eight hours. It wasn't something I would ever do again; the whole experience was disconcerting because I felt so out of control.

That night passed in a frenzy of scratching the dozens of mosquito bites I'd accumulated on my knees, my elbows and my ankles. To make matters worse I was sunburned – I'd forgotten to slap on enough sunblock before taking the acid – and we had nothing to ease the pain. In the morning we asked if there was a doctor on the island. There wasn't, but we were told about a nurse who dispensed first aid. We found her office, and she took one look at my shoulders and declared them first-degree burns. I spent the rest of the holiday keeping them out of the water, sporting two large gauze dressings taped on like white epaulettes with my Zandra Rhodes shorts – not quite the stylish beach ensemble I had imagined.

Back in London, Zandra was sympathetic when we went round to her and Alex's flat for supper, something we did every Saturday night we were in London. They used to have massive fights – we once arrived to find him bashing her on the arm with a three-pin plug while she was ripping up his Fair Isle sweater – because they were in a difficult business, fashion, and at the cutting edge of it, so finances were tight and Zandra was unused to modifying her ideas to cut costs. Her designs used yards and yards of hand-printed silks and chiffons, and took hours of handwork to finish, as beads, feathers and stitching were added. I had been given a peach printed felt coat which must have had half a dozen yards in the circular skirt. It was tied with long silk strings threaded with beads, a real museum piece.

Like Zandra, Alex had studied fabric design at the RCA. He went on to sell his work to Mary Quant, but he soon took a job as a set designer for Thames Television. His design abilities were apparent the minute you walked through the front door of their ground-floor flat in Notting Hill Gate. It consisted of just one huge room, from the front to the back of the building, with a bathroom and a small kitchen down the hall. Alex had made a huge circular dining tabletop of Formica, which sat on a ribbed orange plastic base. There was just one long snake-like upholstered seat which curved round it. Alex designed a room for a *Daily Telegraph* feature, and to publicise it I was photographed with him in their front

room, sporting a silvery-green long wig, and sheer chiffon trousers by Zandra.

Alex and Zandra accompanied us to Wales for several weekends in the spring and summer, staying at Tim's family cottage near Tregaron. Zandra astounded the locals with her riot of blue and green hair – she looked like an exotic parrot in blue dungarees, her chipped metallic nail polish, her hands covered in printing inks. We'd spend the time walking, with Tim snapping away continuously and Zandra scribbling in her sketchbooks.

On most Saturdays their fights abated while we ate supper, which was usually pasta and salad, and then Zandra would get out the Black and Decker and finish a bit of woodwork (she was making a dressing table) while we attempted to talk over the sound of an electric saw. Around half past ten we'd walk down to the Electric Cinema on Portobello Road for the late-night show at eleven o'clock, generally a mixed bill of avant-garde movies by people like William Burroughs, Andy Warhol and Kenneth Anger. In Andy's movies very little happened for hours; they might be of people sleeping, or partying and they definitely didn't have a narrative or plot. Burroughs made a film called *Cutups* in which the film had been sliced into sections and randomly spliced together again, putting the dialogue into nonsensical order – it was to have a huge influence on musicians like David Bowie.

Notting Hill at that time was a very cosmopolitan place, not the rich enclave it is today. Back in 1969 Jamaicans still lived there in rented accommodation in the huge crumbling stucco terraces, along with artists like David Hockney and designers like Ossie Clark and Zandra. Portobello Road was a mixture of bustling vegetable market, antiques and really good junk stalls in the area around Goldbourne Road at the far northern end. Donald Cammel and Nicolas Roeg set their outrageous film *Performance*, starring Mick Jagger, round the corner from Zandra's flat.

In May Mick wore a Ossie Clark white frock over jeans when the Stones gave a free concert one Saturday in Hyde Park. We all went, and then crossed the road to spend the evening in the Royal Albert Hall, where Chuck Berry opened the show for the Who. The rockers in the audience were so pissed off that Berry wasn't topping the bill that they heated up pennies with their lighters and then chucked them down from the balcony onto our heads in the arena below – there was pandemonium and the show was nearly stopped by the anxious security men.

The Saturday-night audience at the Electric was much more laid-back. People would smoke dope during the films, then leave their seats to buy a cup of coffee or a bacon sandwich, and be so stoned they couldn't find their way back to their friends. Even worse, the Electric was in a state of considerable disrepair, with numerous seats missing from the stalls, and you often heard a cry of pain as someone tried to sit down in the dark and dropped to the floor, scalding their laps with hot coffee!

Chapter 3

In March 1969 my career as a journalist really began to take off: I moved from *Petticoat* to the *Daily Mail*. My 'A–Z of Living' had been spotted by the *Mail*'s women's editor, Shirley Conran. She called me up and, after we met, offered me a job as deputy fashion editor. I was very flattered and accepted immediately. I was to be part of the 'Femail' team – the *Mail* had launched this new section to entice more women to buy the paper. Although Shirley no longer appeared in the office after I arrived, her PA, Celia Brayfield, occupied a corner desk.

In Shirley's absence, my immediate boss was Sandy Fawkes, a red-haired, tempestuous journalist with a legendary temper and a huge appetite for booze and men – she was to be my mentor and guide throughout my drunken two years at Associated Newspapers. Sandy wore black pleated skirts, white silk blouses, black sparkly tight sweaters, black stockings and high-heeled shoes. She oozed glamour, even in the smoky atmosphere of the back rooms of the bars where we seemed to spend hours every day.

This was a completely different word from *Petticoat*; now there were daily, not weekly, deadlines, and the 'Femail' team had to meet the capricious and sometimes plain weird demands of our male bosses. In between furious bouts of work, rushing out to knock off a fashion picture or attend a photocall, there were hours to kill until we got further instructions from the picture desk or the features editor. I would be asked to photograph men in pin-striped shorts in the City (an un-funny take on the latest craze, 'hot pants') or grill glamorous women about what they were wearing to Ascot. We contributed a story

to the news pages of the paper almost every day, as well as to the weekly 'Femail' section.

Most weekdays, at 1 p.m., Sandy and I walked up the road to El Vino's wine bar, in Fleet Street, where women were not allowed to buy drinks or stand at the bar. We sat at a small round table in the back room with the opera critic from the *Guardian*, Philip Hope-Wallace, the editor of the *Daily Express*, Derek Marks, and various other middle-aged executives who liked nothing more than to stare at my legs and buy me champagne. Sandy, who had been married to the cartoonist Wally 'Trog' Fawkes, was a complete star in this environment, graciously accepting compliments and downing bucketloads of champers without appearing to get pissed.

I was awed by her confidence and ready put-downs. In the office I felt intimidated by unattractive subeditors who were invariably male, white and middle-aged and who wore string vests under their nylon shirts. Senior executives just slavered over me. Sandy taught me how to stand my ground and win. It was 1971, and I had only been married for four years, but already I'd lost all notion of being faithful. There was so much happening in my life, from music to film to fashion – Tim and I lived in a whirlwind of exhibition openings, parties and events. On paper (and in photos) we seemed the perfect couple – with so many shared interests – but I'd had several affairs within a couple of years of being married. I was too young to be tied down. On the *Mail* I learned how to exploit my youth, my striking appearance and my opinions to full effect.

On Fridays my day assumed a different ritual. I would get up at seven and file copy by noon. Then Sandy and I would take a taxi to the French pub on Dean Street, drinking till two, when we'd repair to Wheelers in Old Compton Street for oysters and Sancerre. Sometimes we were joined by Francis Bacon, which was always very intimidating. He'd only want to talk about face cream and hair dye – he told me he used the cheapest Boots lotions and his tousled dark brown hair was achieved with boot polish! Francis could veer from one extreme to the other very quickly. He would find me entertaining and then tire of the conversation, telling everyone in earshot to fuck off the drunker he got. We'd retreat up the road to Muriel's Colony Room for a further couple of hours' boozing.

One afternoon an elderly man sitting on the banquette

at the back of the bar suddenly took his hat off, was silently sick into it, put it back on his head and made a stylish exit. I never forgot that. Another time the actress Adrienne Corri arrived with two men she'd met at lunch. Soon they became tiresome, so she emptied a bottle of champagne over the head of one, with the retort: 'You've bored me all the fucking way from Knightsbridge, and you're still boring me, so fuck off.' Which they did. Muriel, perched on her stool at the end of the bar, with her helmet of dark hair and permanent cigarette, greeted everyone she loved in the same way: 'Hello, cunty.' Ian Board, behind the bar, kept the conversation going, together with endless drinks paid for by the latest sucker to be lured through the door.

At six o'clock, I'd stagger back down the road to the French pub and then, around eight, descend to the basement room that was Gerry's private members' club – known to its devotees as 'Losers' Lounge' – a few doors further down the street. Here, Jeffrey Barnard would be grumpily mouthing off to all and sundry. It was his first port of call after being hospitalized on several occasions. By nine, the manager, Shaun, would put me in a minicab home. I would walk through the door, unable to cook dinner, let alone eat anything, stagger to bed and sleep it all off. Sometimes the drinking varied a bit. It might start at the 'Stab in the Back' pub (the White Hart) next to the *Daily Mirror* or the 'Mucky Duck' (the Swan) by the *Daily Mail*. We might convene at 4 p.m. in the Crossed Keys in Fleet Street by the *Daily Express*, and then progress to the Kismet, a drinking club in Covent Garden where the clientele was a mixture of plain-clothes policemen from Bow Street and scene-shifters and lighting technicians from Covent Garden. Then, at six o'clock, we'd roll into the Wig and Pen club opposite the Law Courts on the Strand. By the age of 23 I had drunk at every single club and pub within a mile of my office. I had successfully completed my initiation into Fleet Street by proving I had stamina and a ready wit, and didn't suffer fools.

After I had been at the *Mail* a few months, the features editor thought I should be given a small space to write a column on Saturdays. Putting together the fashion pages was easy, but writing a column was definitely not – I was not confident as a writer, and although I had a quick line in repartee at the pub (probably developed in self-defence, given the way I looked) I found expressing myself in print difficult. I felt I was being used as the in-house 'youth' mascot, and my column didn't represent what I really felt or thought: it was something I manufactured to order to please the editor, who badly wanted to be seen to be in touch with fashionable London.

What the *Mail* wanted was a diary of what was happening in Chelsea, the epicentre of fashion, so they called my column 'SW3'. After a couple of months, thankfully, this got dropped and I was able to write a more general column under my by-line about my (to them) 'wacky' lifestyle. It is excruciatingly embarrassing to read it today.

In 1970 Tim got a real break from another photographer called John Vaughn, who wrote about architecture and design for the upmarket monthly glossy magazine *Queen*. John liked Tim's work and asked him to contribute some stories. The first was to be shot in Paris, and we went over for the weekend – I was thrilled because it meant another opportunity to scour the fleamarkets for my new craze, art deco. I went to the huge street markets at Porte de Montreuil and Porte de Vanves, both on the Boulevard Périphérique, and spent hours picking through piles of stuff and haggling like mad – we didn't have much spare cash. I bought large decorative ceramic fish, marquetry boxes and trays, beautiful blue glass bowls moulded with fish swimming around them, pieces of velvet furnishing fabrics and jewellery.

We really hit it off with Emmanuelle Khanh and her Vietnamese husband, Quasar, who we met when Tim was commissioned to photograph his blow-up furniture. They lived in a large apartment near the Luxembourg gardens, which was totally white, furnished with Quasar's designs. Tim decided to photograph Quasar's inflatable chairs, settee and table floating in an Olympic-sized swimming pool on the outskirts of Paris. Quasar was totally enthusiastic, making all the arrangements. The pool was deserted – it was a Sunday morning – and the pictures were extraordinary. That night, we climbed into their square perspex car, a box fitted onto the chassis of a Mini Moke, and revelled in the astonished stares from passers-by as Quasar drove us up to the Champs Elysées to a cinema which specialised in horror movies to see George Romero's *Night of the Living Dead*, a black-and-white epic in which flesh-eating people surround a small wooden house and attempt to finish off the terrified occupants (I had nightmares about it for months afterwards). Later, we had supper at a chic nightclub on the Left Bank.

Emmanuelle was extremely charming, and rather shy. Her designs were tailored and very precise, and she created beautiful linen blouses and skirts with delicate stitching. She always wore huge white glasses, sometimes encrusted with rhinestones – her trademark. Soon, I too had a pair.

Tim's pictures were well received and we managed to get an assignment to work together – we planned a trip to Japan to cover the huge architectural fair in Osaka, Expo 70. Japan was considered rather cut off from contemporary culture in those days, and I was really looking forward to seeing what impact the building of dozens of pavilions by the world's top architects would have. Although nominally a celebration of trade, Expo exhibitions had always been a chance for each country to try and outdo the next with innovative designs, the most notable being the extraordinary molecular structure put up for the Brussels Expo in 1964, the Atomium, and Expo 70 was to be no different, with an optimistic theme of 'progress and harmony for mankind'. We would be staying in Kyoto, a short train ride from the site outside

Osaka, and planned a few days in Tokyo at the end of the trip.

The flight to Osaka was interminable, not helped by the fact that the passengers on the flight – organised by my old college, the Architectural Association – were mostly architects, and had managed to drink the plane dry by the time we stopped to refuel in Anchorage. Some of them had lied to their wives about the time the flight actually left London, in order to start the party before they took off!

In Kyoto, our days soon took on a pattern. We avoided the drunken architects, some of whom seemed to spend all their time in the working men's clubs, where customers sat at benches drinking and women wearing no knickers walked up and down long tables between them. We'd catch the train to the Expo site (and working out which train to board when we were confronted with a language made up of symbols that meant nothing to us was fraught, to say the least) and then spend the day walking around the huge exhibition area, marvelling at the pavilions, which ranged from the futuristic to the makeshift. There were many domes of varying sizes, including the American pavilion, clearly inspired by

Buckminster Fuller. There were mirrored pyramids housing escalators and exhibition spaces, monorails, giant silvered space frames with steel ribs, and large, windy piazzas. It was like a film set from a science-fiction movie. Over the next few months, an astonishing 64 million people visited the site (before it closed in September) of which 97 percent were Japanese!

Soon I realised, that I, too, was one of the attractions to the locals. The Queen had opened the British pavilion the previous month, but now the bulk of the visitors were not sophisticated international jet-setters, but large groups of ordinary working-class Japanese men and women, who arrived by coach from all over the country, often from remote rural areas. It was the first time many of them had seen Westerners in any numbers, and they couldn't believe how tall I was. Wearing an old fur coat I'd picked up down Portobello Road for a fiver (it was bitterly cold and windy), bright green suede knee-length boots, and a rainbow knitted Peruvian hat over my pink-and-green-striped hair, I must have looked completely bizarre. The Japanese visitors soon started to form queues in front of me, waving pieces of paper for me to sign, and gesticulating that they would like to have their pictures taken. Perhaps they thought I was a trainee sumo wrestler from another planet. Who knows?

We spent afternoons walking up and down the narrow back lanes of Kyoto, buying china rice bowls and blue-and-white-striped cotton sleeping robes. We left our Western-style hotel and moved into a traditional inn, where we had a large suite with tatami mats on the floor and sliding parchment screens. We learned how to bath Japanese-style, soaping, scrubbing and washing ourselves, cleaning the soap off with a shower hose, and then sinking into a deep hot tub where you could sit and relax for hours. We had supper in our room, sitting crosslegged on cushions, eating a selection of sushi and sashimi served by simpering girls in formal kimonos. I was completely captivated.

We visited the Zen Buddhist sect's Ryoan-ji temple, where the exquisite formal gardens consisted of beautifully raked sand, a few perfectly positioned pebbles and some isolated Japanese maple trees. The garden was unlike anything I had ever seen before, and I began to understand a new way of looking at things which was completely imbued with meaning and stillness – not

concepts which had much currency in my version of Swinging London.

On the train to Expo one morning, a man in priest's robes tried to strike up a conversation in halting English. On discovering that we were a photographer and a journalist, he asked us to come and see his temple, telling us that it was extremely unusual. Intrigued, we got off at his stop and followed him through the crowded streets to a large compound. Through an impressive arch, across an open space, up some wide dark wooden steps, then we left our shoes at the entrance to the shrine itself, and walked into a large dark room made of polished wood. The priest explained that this temple was considered remarkable because the monks who had built it had decided to construct a 'musical' floor. Using planks of different length in different woods, they had built a surface of highly polished timber about 50 feet square. As we walked across it, the boards made a variety of infinitely subtly varying sounds – for me the whole experience summed up the best of the Japanese approach to life. I was taken to a small room and given a pen and a sheet of paper – would I write my experience of the temple down for their newsletter?

Back in London, Tim and I were commissioned to work together again, for *Queen*. The editor was an extremely eccentric American called Fred Grunfeld, who became a very close friend. He was a former editor of *Time* magazine, who had a formidable knowledge of classical music and was writing a scholarly biography of Berlioz. He had a house in the village of Deya, on the north coast of Majorca, where the poet Robert Graves had gone to live. In London Fred rented a studio apartment in a Georgian terraced house some way east of Tower Bridge, in Limehouse. His long, narrow living space looked out onto the river and half a dozen large empty barges were moored outside. A woman who worked in films lived upstairs, and the ground floor was a barge-repair shop.

The house was owned by Dorothy Woodward Fisher, the only woman barge-owner on the whole Thames, who also owned the house next door (where the writer Dan Farson was living) and the large barge yard down the road. Fred's flat was very atmospheric, a room with just a bed and sofas, with the end entirely glass, opening on to a wooden balcony over the water.

While Tim continued to photograph architecture and the odd fashion spread for *Queen*, I contributed to a piece about the mini versus the new maxi-length skirt, alongside an article by the American feminist writer Gloria Steinem, and wrote another about new ways of living – it featured the architect Peter Cook and his 'media trolley' and some 'bathing pods' designed by Nick Grimshaw and Terry Farrell. In August Tim and I spent a couple of weeks on Majorca, staying at Fred's house. Deya was relatively unspoiled; apart from the extended Graves family, some American writers had settled there. Summer brought an influx of Spanish families into the mix, and the small pebbly beach was packed. I would walk high above the village of Sóller and towards Valldemossa on old mule tracks through ancient olive groves which shimmered silvery-green in the intense heat.

Back in London the refuse collectors went on strike and the streets were piled high with rubbish. When we took the train from Kings Cross up to Northumberland for the weekend, the waiter in the dining car suddenly went mad and chucked a large dish of peas and potatoes all over us. It was his last journey after 25 years and he'd had a drink or three – and had clearly been dying to do that to a passenger for some time. I couldn't really blame him, and we all laughed off the incident. The train conductor must have taken a different view, though, because our waiter was taken off the train by the police when we arrived in York.

At Christmas Tim and I made our own cards by taking a series of pictures in which our bodies formed the letters 'Happy Xmas'. It was the next stage in a long tradition of DIY cards which had started with our wedding invitation back in 1967.

It was 9.55 a.m. and I was in the ladies' lavatory of the *Daily Mail* on the first floor of Carmelite House, just off

Fleet Street. I had come to work from Chelsea, and my journey had been eventful. First of all I stood at the bus stop in the Fulham Road just along from our flat and waited ten minutes for a number 22 to South Kensington Underground station. Various cars hooted, and I ignored the catcalls. My hair was razor cut, with a bright yellow star dyed on the crown. I wore green opaque tights and tartan platform-soled shoes by Manolo Blahnik which made me about six foot three inches tall. My workwear consisted of a pair of small pink and red knitted shorts and matching sweater, topped with a peppermint-green sleeveless goatskin jacket from Dorothée Bis in Paris.

I ran down the stairs at South Kensington to catch the train to Blackfriars, not realising my footwear made me higher than the door of the carriage. I hit my head so hard that I lay sprawled on the floor like a DayGlo ostrich. The other passengers smirked and averted their gaze as I reassembled myself, dusted my legs and hung onto an overhead strap.

Now, in the calm of the ladies' lavatory, I was systematically teasing my hair into tufts, gluing on my false eyelashes and applying pale pink lipstick. Lynda Lee-Potter carefully ignored me, unwrapping her blond hair from a series of large rollers and back-combing it into a perfect bob. She had arrived, as usual, on the train from Bournemouth, wearing a long black cloak with a hood which concealed not only her body but also the fact that nine large plastic rollers were firmly clipped to her scalp. She wore a white blouse which fastened right up to the neck, with a pie-crust frill round it, and a long, black skirt. Lynda never revealed any flesh whatsoever – we used to wonder whether she actually had legs at all. Her look was that of demure supplicant.

Lynda represented everything I loathed. She had a soft, pseudo-genteel accent, fluttered her eyelashes a lot, and was relentlessly feminine, which was one way of dealing with the men who ran the *Daily Mail*. She was being groomed for stardom as a feature writer and columnist, while I was the resident weirdo, the deputy fashion editor who wrote a short, humorous column every Saturday. I was just 22 years old, and to me Lynda seemed from another world, where men were in charge and women did their bidding.

When I'd been at the *Mail* for two years we were called to a staff meeting and told by the management that the bosses planned to reduce the newspaper in size from broadsheet to tabloid, and that many redundancies would result. I had heard on the grapevine that the *Evening Standard* were looking for a deputy for Suzy Menkes, their fashion editor, who was pregnant, and I landed the job after a frightening interview with the editor, Charles Wintour, who had a glacial manner and spoke like a Dalek. In spite of this, he turned out to be one of my biggest champions, and I was promised a bigger space for a column in their Saturday paper, alongside legendary pop columnist Ray Connolly.

The 'night of the long knives' soon arrived, when the management of the *Daily Mail* summoned staff to their offices one at a time, and handed out brown envelopes which contained Xeroxed letters telling you whether you'd been sacked or not. A raucous party atmosphere prevailed in the Mucky Duck, led by the film critic Barry Norman and by Sandy, who flirted outrageously with several of her male colleagues. It felt more like a wedding than a wake. To my great joy I was one of those made redundant, and my little bit of paper promised me the grand total of five months' money – one month for every year I'd worked, and my notice period of three months. Sandy was delighted to be fired as well – she'd already lined up a job as fashion editor of the *Daily Express*. Only the simperers were spared. When one of them approached Sandy and said in a querulous voice, 'I wonder why they didn't sack me?' Sandy retorted, 'Because you were the fucking cheapest, love.' Exit the journalist concerned in floods of tears, to general pleasure.

My office at the *Standard* was on the top floor of the paper's building in Shoe Lane, just off Holborn Circus. I reached it by walking through the greyhound results office, and gave the middle-aged blokes a treat every morning when I arrived in a short skirt and platform-soled boots. Suzy Menkes was a formidable boss, dictatorial, ruthless, extremely organised. We got on very well, to general astonishment. First of all, she was quick to spot that I didn't want her job, and that I would work hard while she was away and her pages wouldn't suffer. She realised that my ambitions lay outside fashion ultimately, and she and I formed a good working relationship and a respect that survives to this day.

Suzy was happily married and so, allegedly, was I. It was 1971 and my life was a round of parties, fashion shows and photo sessions. Sandy went to cover the Paris couture collections and I was allocated a huge suite at the Tremoille Hotel. I was so drunk I remember trying to dye my hair pink and squirting Krazy Colour on the marble tiles round the bath. I spent hours trying to rub it off with flannels and soap, fearful I might be landed with a mammoth bill on my expenses! The couture collections were hard work, starting at 9 a.m. and with up to eight shows a day, during which time I was expected to file copy over the telephone at least three times, spelling out every last bit of punctuation. I caused general outrage at Balenciaga and dreary Molyneux by turning up in pink denim dungarees with my hair dyed to match. The French journalists hissed but I couldn't give a fuck – I was photographed by *Women's Wear Daily* for their style section.

In London I hung out with designers and artists, and my look was of the moment. Couture clothes seemed a redundant statement from another era, and the *Evening Standard* picture desk was continually moaning that the models didn't show enough flesh! They were spoilt with all the hot pants and minis on parade daily on the streets of London. Instead of computers, we used manual typewriters to write our copy on bits of paper which rows of (nearly all male) subeditors would correct – and mangle. The newspaper was set in hot metal by printers in the composing room on the first floor, a macho den you entered at your peril.

Sandy and I still met several times a week, but I was beginning to realise that I couldn't cope with this much booze on a regular basis. Although I adored Sandy, in some ways she was becoming a liability, a drunk who repeated herself endlessly, told the same stories over and over again. Was I doing the same? What kind of message did I send out by hanging out with her? One lunchtime I went to a wine bar around the corner from the *Standard* with a couple of friends, including some journalists from the *Mirror* – we were all having dinner at an Italian restaurant later, with our spouses. Around five one of them asked me to meet him at his flat after work. It would more convenient, he said, and we could go on to supper together.

When I arrived at the mansion block I rang the bell and went up several floors. He opened the door and showed me into a book-lined living room. There was no one else there – I'd been really stupid. He threw himself on me, tried to tear my clothes off, kissed me and told me he was desperate to have sex with me. I was stunned. I couldn't imagine why this man thought I'd have sex with him. Actually, I'd been having an affair with a colleague of his for two years, but no one knew – I couldn't imagine that my lover, who we were also meeting for dinner, would have let anyone in on our secret. I dashed down the corridor of the flat, with my unwanted suitor in hot pursuit. The front door was double-locked and he grabbed me and started groping again. I pushed him away and told him he'd made a big mistake. Luckily, he realised I would have physically trounced him, and in a fury he unlocked the door. I ran down the stairs.

I took a taxi home, where Tim was patiently waiting for us to go out to dinner. 'I'm sorry,' I said, 'I have a really bad migraine. Do you mind going without me?' He agreed, and I didn't speak to the man who attacked me again, until ten years later. He was very good-looking, charming and urbane; still is. But I never wanted to have sex with anyone who looked like that. I only find problem men attractive.

In Muriel's one day a couple of years later I met Sandy's friend John Hurt, who had just finished filming the television drama *The Naked Civil Servant*, in which he played the famous raconteur and legendary camp icon Quentin Crisp, with dyed red hair, exactly the same shade as mine. Tim was away shooting in Milan and soon John (he had no idea I was married) and I were back at my house in bed. An amiable drunk, he was totally captivating and charming. Another time I embarked on an affair with the son of a famous painter, a champion oarsman. There was nothing he liked more than having sex in his bedroom at his parents' house in Regent's Park, with me wearing my new wolf fur coat, under all his trophies hung on the wall. After he contracted hepatitis during a competition in Egypt, I sneaked into his room at the Tropical Diseases Hospital in Camden for afternoon sex, pretending to my office I was out on appointments. When he recovered and coached the Oxford University rowing team to success in the Boat Race, I followed in a launch, cheering them on. These affairs were nothing more than flings, just fun diversions from the grind of work on a daily paper.

But I was beginning to realise that, after four years of drinking, I would have to cut loose from Sandy. My friends outside Fleet Street were completely separate, and it was difficult to reconcile the two ways of behaving.

The designers like Zandra worked so hard; they were determined to be successful, no matter how many hours it required. Tim, too, was travelling all over Europe taking pictures for *Vogue* and *Queen*, as well as the architectural press. They were disciplined virtual non-drinkers who regarded my world, where people disappeared for hours on end and emerged sloshed to hunch over a keyboard and churn out copy to an imminent deadline, as completely weird.

Gradually I stopped seeing Sandy, stopped returning her calls. Occasionally I'd run in to her, still in glamorous black, now living in a small flat in St James, off Piccadilly. But she no longer worked for the *Express*. She'd lost her job in a staff cull, and had to freelance. She was short of cash, and a pathetic figure. She went to America and freelanced there, eventually meeting a man (who was briefly her lover) who had committed a series of murders. Naturally she wrote a book about it! Then it was back to the tiny flat and drinking every day in Soho until her death.

Tim and I were enjoying our new circle of friends and I was working hard, but feeling under the weather. I wasn't ill, but was increasingly suffering from debilitating chronic headaches, which had started in 1965 when I was on holiday in Cornwall with Rex, the fiancé I dumped. I'd been staying at Patrick Heron's house outside St Ives, when I felt as if someone had plunged a knife through my head. I literally fell on the floor and I spent that evening and the next day in bed. Since then the headaches had increased in intensity – sometimes making my eyes water and the base of my neck tighten so much I could barely move my head.

I'd had all sorts of tests for blood clots on the brain. One took place in a rather imposing, grim building off Cheyne Walk in Chelsea where a nurse rubbed my scalp with thick Vaseline and put on my head a tight black rubber cap, to which they attached electrodes. Then I received a series of mild electric impulses, and coloured pencils attached to the wires produced the most exquisite coloured map of my brain-waves. The upshot of all this was that the specialist told me I wasn't epileptic, I didn't have any kind of brain damage, there were no aneurisms or areas of extraordinary pressure in my skull. In short, I appeared to have classic migraine. I was told to keep a note of headaches and write down what I'd done and what I'd eaten, in the hope of working out what triggered the attacks. Tim bought me a beautiful black and gold diary from Biba and we named it the Headache Annual.

All well and good, but some days I would have to leave the *Daily Mail*'s or *Evening Standard*'s offices, walk up to Charterhouse Square off Smithfield Market and register at the Migraine Clinic, where they sedated me with pills or an injection and I spent up to six hours sleeping in a darkened room instead of writing my column or filing copy. I tried avoiding cheese, chocolate and sherry. I took enormous quantities of painkillers, sometimes ten over-the-counter ones like aspirin in a day, three days or more a week.

I went to see a nice doctor called Wilfred Barlow in a mansion block by the Royal Albert Hall. He was the leading exponent of something called the Alexander Technique, which involved learning a series of spinal stretching exercises and a better way of standing and sitting to improve your posture. He felt that all my pain was derived from my appalling slouch – he might have been right, but I only managed half a dozen sessions on his couch. During the parts of the consultation when I was supposed to be channelling all my mental energy into 'thinking tall through the top of my skull', I'd be making shopping lists and trying to decide what to write my column about that week.

I gave up on the Alexander Technique, just as I'd realised that the teachings of Meher Baba would never work for me. I tried to read the new Penguin paperback about Zen Buddhism, but gave up after a couple of chapters. I was definitely not a spiritual person at this stage of my life. I was someone who shopped, was passionate about fashion, went to clubs and art galleries, loved talking to friends, partying and crossing cities and countries in search of street markets and art deco bargains, haggling for them in French and Spanish. I was not the kind of person who could meditate for five minutes to achieve mental calm or a higher philosophical plane. I settled for a regime of painkillers, supplemented with Ativan tranquillisers; sometimes I took about four a day – anything to deaden the pain. My doctor said, 'One day you'll just grow out of the headaches,' which didn't offer much comfort as he didn't suggest a time scale.

During my time at the *Mail* and *Standard*, Tim and I continued seeing old friends like Mike and Kate McInnery, and made many new ones. Among the latter was a neighbour in Chelsea, the pop artist Allen Jones and his very pretty wife, Janet. We met through Patrick Heron, whose London flat was in Edith Grove, less than a quarter of a mile from ours on the Fulham Road. Allen and Janet lived next door to Patrick, and they were also friends with the artist Joe Tilson, who had been one of my tutors at college. Joe and his wife, Jos, had now moved down to Wiltshire, as had several other successful artists like Howard Hodgkin, Peter Blake and Richard Smith, and it marked the end of an era in the London pop art scene.

In spite of their very different styles and approaches to their work – Patrick was an abstract artist who used large seductive blobs of colour symbolising the intense colours of the landscape at the western end of the Cornish peninsula, where he lived, whereas Allen's inspiration was pure pop: objects like buses, shoes, women, the stuff he saw every day in London – they were good friends. Both men were highly intellectual, voracious readers and consumers of culture, both great conversationalists and social animals.

Allen seemed emaciated, with thinning hair and a worried-looking face. Janet was his perfect muse, with shoulder-length blond hair, a great figure, and legs that could stop the traffic, usually shown to perfection in the smallest of miniskirts or hot pants. She was always in the background, cooking, keeping the house running like clockwork, uncomplaining and good-natured, dealing with their many dinner guests and a stream of visitors, offering tea, coffee, home cooking. Allen had met Janet when he was her tutor at Croydon art school, and now they were the proud parents of identical small twin girls, Sara and Thea.

Allen drew, painted and photographed Janet endlessly – she appeared in almost all his work in one form or another, and it wasn't suprising that he was a huge fan of those American graphic artists who drew perfect poster girls, Vargas and Petty. Allen had left the Royal College of

Art after a year, but had gone on to win the Young Artist prize at the Paris Biennale in 1963. He was an excellent draughtsman and watercolourist. Janet was a very good cook, and soon we were spending a couple of evenings a week at their house in Edith Grove. Janet and I would talk about fashion, while Tim and Allen planned a project together, a limited-edition book entitled *Waitress*. Allen was always getting all sorts of weird fetish costumes made for Janet; she didn't mind posing in them at home for him to paint, but wasn't that thrilled to be seen wearing them in public.

In 1969 Allen had decided to move on to sculpture, and a pneumatic life-sized woman was made, loosely based on Janet, wearing a green leather corset with bare breasts and high-heeled lace-up boots. In one version she had her arms open, palms upwards, forming a hat-stand. In another she knelt on all fours, her breasts swinging free, facing the floor, and peering into a mirror. On her back she supported a sheet of glass with sandblasted edges, cut into the shape of a palette. This was a 'coffee table'. When they were exhibited there was uproar. Feminists complained that Allen was denigrating and debasing the female form – he thought it was a witty joke. Either way, the limited edition sold out, and Allen had well and truly grown out of the 'pop artist' tag, which he found somewhat passé.

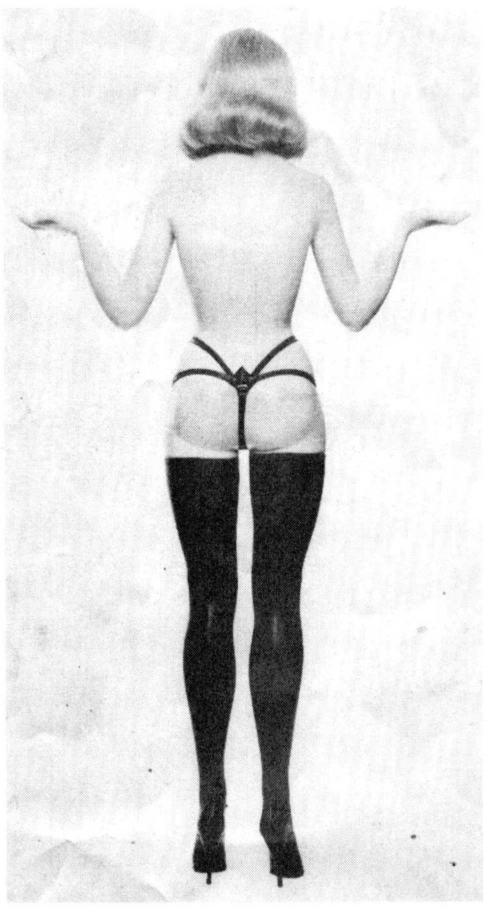

Over the next couple of years Tim and Allen's *Waitress* project took the hat-stand one stage further. Tim photographed Janet in a specially made black rubber waitress costume. It was skin-tight, with black rubber leggings and high-heeled boots. Her breasts were covered, but when she turned round her backside was completely bare! The poor girl spent hours in this get-up being photographed in every conceivable pose by Tim: bending over, serving tea, holding a tray and taking an order. Then the two men went all over the place selecting restaurant and café interiors, from Fortnum & Mason's in Piccadilly, to Derry & Tom's Rainbow Room in Kensington, to the Charing Cross Hotel and a burger bar opposite the Roundhouse, which Tim photographed in black and white. Finally, the fetishistic waitress (Janet, with her hair scraped back into a severe bun) was photo-montaged into these hostelries, in appropriately unlikely poses. The best one was of her sitting on the counter of a café in Blenheim Crescent off the Portobello Road, which ended up in the *Daily Mirror*.

Allen produced a couple of prints of a waitress for the front and back of the book, which was bound in red leather with the most beautiful marbled endpapers. An edition of 125 was published in 1972, all numbered and signed, and sold out at £125 a copy. A later edition was produced for the Japanese market, bound in green.

Allen decided to make a print of me for the cover of the art magazine *Studio International*. He removed my

glasses, scraped my hair back and painted my face like a Zulu princess's, with tribal markings in bright colours. Later he made me a thank-you gift by tearing up a dozen of the prints and making them into a fan-shaped collage, gluing it onto a canvas and signing it 'A fan of JSP'!

He was highly inventive – a complete obsessive. He made one-off menus to mark the suppers we had together, collages of our holidays together in the South of France and Morocco and special events. Like Tim (and, to a certain degree, me) he lived, breathed, slept and ate work. But Tim and Allen were already established in their fields of photography and art, whereas I was just starting in journalism, and knew it would be some time before I wrote anything I would be really proud of. For the moment, I preferred to lap up whatever experiences I could, from exhibitions to concerts to the cinema to books.

Chapter 4

It was around nine in the evening, and the bed was a complete mess: not only were the sheets and blankets everywhere, but they were strewn with pieces of smelly white paper and bits of uneaten fish and chips. An HP Sauce bottle lay on the floor. Outside, it was a chilly October evening, and on the river there was little activity, except for the blue flashing light of a river police launch en route to the Isle of Dogs. The only sounds were the groaning of the empty barges moored outside the house, as they rose and fell with the movement of the water, and the whistle of the wind against the windows. It was a shame to draw the blinds, but I didn't want our neighbours to be able to peek into the room from their terrace.

Doug was lying with his eyes half closed, smoking, using one of my art deco dishes as an ashtray – cigarettes were a habit I detested but was willing to overlook in his case. No one could call the man in the bed skinny. He was roly-poly round the middle, starting to lose his hair, pushing forty and with a face that looked a bit squashed. But he was one of the funniest people I'd ever met, and through his patronage I'd acquired a whole new circle of friends. We weren't really having an affair – his lazy lovemaking was far too laid-back to call it that – just the occasional bit of fun.

I was working hard: rushing around London going to designer shows and art galleries and photographing up to eight pages of fashion a week for the *Evening Standard*, as well as writing my Saturday column. I can't remember how I met Doug Hayward – it was probably through journalists we both knew – but we really hit it off, and soon we were having lunch or a drink regularly. He was a tailor, with a shop in Mount Street, and his list of clients was like a roll-call of fashionable London. He'd started his career just off Fulham Broadway, near where I'd been born and grown up, so we immediately had west London in common.

Like my father, Doug was a devoted follower of Fulham Football Club, and now that they'd sunk to the second division he led a posse of fellow devotees – among them the actor Rodney Bewes, advertising executive Peter Shillingford and soon me – to the home games every fortnight. We'd start with lunch (which Doug, who was fanatically careful with money, had negotiated for the bargain price of a fiver) at Alvaro's Aretusa club on the Kings Road – pasta and loads of red wine. Then we'd drive down to Craven Cottage and take our seats in the stands to watch Rodney Marsh, George Best and Bobbie Moore try to recreate Fulham's glory days.

My father was always at the games – I usually bought him a season ticket as a birthday or Christmas present – but in block D, as far away from us as possible. Dad was appalled by our repartee and jeering. When yachts went past on the river behind the stands we'd all shout, 'Jaws!' and we passed the boring stretches of games with singsongs and chanting. My father took Fulham Football Club very seriously and wouldn't even acknowledge that the woman in a fur coat made of wolfskins dyed blue, green and red was a blood relative – we arrived at and left the ground separately.

Tim and I were now living in Limehouse, in east London, in a Georgian sea captain's house, on the other side of the city from the neighbourhood where I'd spent my childhood in a terraced house off Parson's Green Lane. We'd spent a whole year looking for somewhere to live – there'd been no more improvements we could make to

our old flat. One of the benefits of the Fulham Road location had been that you could see about half of Chelsea's football pitch, if you stood on the toilet with the bathroom window open, but few visitors were that keen.

The little room off our kitchen had been Tim's darkroom, with the result that the whole flat smelt of chemicals. After a while he'd found a proper base to work from and shared a studio at the top of Drury Lane with another aspiring photographer, Steve Hiett, and printing was done there or at a lab. The former darkroom became a guest room, but soon we'd tired of people who outstayed their welcome (and London at the end of the 1960s was certainly a great place to visit) so we'd raised the floor, carpeted it with green fake grass, strewn it with cushions and renamed it 'the nook', a spot for a quiet read, or perhaps a one-night stay – it wasn't that inviting. The kitchen had a table and two chairs made from cardboard, left over from one of my photo shoots. There was an ancient gas cooker we'd bought in Earls Court and carried home in pieces through Brompton Cemetery as we couldn't afford a removal van.

Our lodger, George, had long gone, of course, and we slept in his old room on a waterbed I'd bought on a whim in Whiteleys sale in September 1971 for £50. It sat in a large wooden box, and had taken several hours to fill from the bath using a long piece of hose. The first night after it was installed, I had drunk a few Bloody Marys and the incessant wave movement (every time one of us turned over, it wobbled) brought on extreme nausea: I was soon throwing up my supper down the toilet. The bed proved a most effective way of cutting back my alcohol intake, and making love on it was pretty scary, because you were liable to build up serious ripples which were very hard to stop! We soon purchased a heater for the waterbed as it felt cold and clammy no matter how many blankets we piled on. Friends came round to marvel at this new oddity, and the cleaning lady left a very sad note one day saying she'd tried to move the bed to vacuum under it, but had been unable to lift it! No wonder: it must have weighed a ton when full of water.

The other small bedroom was used as our office and was full of books, filing cabinets and storage stuff. The front room held our art deco three-piece suite and the octagonal sleeping platform we'd built from wood found in skips, now used as extra seating. This room was dominated by a seven-foot plywood cutout of an extremely dapper Tony Curtis in a white suit, which we'd stolen from outside the cinema in Leicester Square during the premiere of *The Great Race*.

But the flat had exhausted its decorating possibilities for us, besides which we still had bad memories of the two drugs raids in '67 and '68. Now it was 1971 and the property boom was under way, with the result that soaring prices meant we couldn't afford anywhere in fashionable Notting Hill Gate or Holland Park, near friends like Zandra and Alex. We'd only managed to save a couple of thousand pounds towards a mortgage, which wasn't going to get us very far.

In July 1971 I went back to my old school, Lady Margaret's Grammar, in Parsons Green, to give a talk. It was Speech Day, and my brief contribution followed others given by old girls who had become teachers, nurses and volunteer workers in Africa. Even though I was the first person from the school to study architecture, and the first old girl who had a column in a national newspaper (quite an achievement for someone not yet 25), I felt I was regarded by the staff as something of a flop. My career wasn't 'worthy' enough for them, and the way I was introduced seemed rather patronising, as if journalism wasn't a real job.

I was very serious about making a successful career in the media, and had appeared on the radio regularly, on shows like *The World at One* with William Hardcastle, Jack de Manio's *Today* show (he was an amiable eccentric, if a bit of a drunk) and the *PM* show at teatime, all on Radio Four. Nonetheless, after my hour at Lady Margaret's I swore I would never again put myself in the humiliating position of being made to feel inferior. One of the staff actually said to me at the tea afterwards, 'I know you think we hated you, but we didn't. We just regarded you as a challenge.' I never forgot that they'd told my mother to take me to elocution lessons – luckily she'd ignored this superfluous piece of advice, and my career had hardly suffered as a result, although my 'common' accent wasn't exactly welcomed by many radio listeners and I'd started to receive hate mail.

Tim and I still saw our old friends in Bristol from time to time, and shortly after moving to Limehouse we drove down to a party there in his latest car, a beautiful grey old Porsche – I still couldn't drive. When we got to Bristol, our pals announced that, as the best hotel in the area was full, they'd booked us into the worst one as a joke. It wouldn't matter, we replied, we were only going to be crashing out late, anyway.

When we got to the place, it was in a double-fronted Edwardian villa in the suburbs. The owners' quarters were to the left of the entrance hall, with their living room bisected by a large dresser placed diagonally, with a television set on it. Behind the dresser, in full view, were a bath and toilet. Our room had a door which stopped about six inches short of the floor and didn't lock. We had to jam all the furniture up against it, and were kept awake all night long by doors opening and closing and men coming and going – we were clearly staying in the local whorehouse!

That autumn our great friend the columnist Christopher Ward married a very pretty model, Fanny, and the service was held at St Columba's Church, Pont Street. Christopher wrote for the *Daily Mirror* and *Petticoat*, was good-looking and amusing, with the same long hair as Tim, and was extremely skilled at networking – he seemed to know everyone from Shirley Conran to politicians, actors, writers and designers. I wore a Jean Muir red silk jersey outfit which consisted of tiny knickers with elastic around the bottom, a flowing empire-line top with full sleeves, and tartan platform-soled shoes. The groom's mother was definitely not amused by my hot pants in the church and pointedly looked the other way. I couldn't have cared less; I knew I had great legs and I got loads of compliments.

After the ceremony we all went to supper and a party at the Aretusa, and everyone from Doug Hayward to David Bailey and Terry O'Neill was there. Next morning, nursing a bit of a hangover, I was astonished to be woken by the phone ringing – it was Christopher calling from the bridal suite at Claridge's. The bride and groom had tried to persuade us to spend the night in the butler's bedroom when we'd gone back for drinks in the early hours of the morning, but we were having none of it. Now Christopher had a real dilemma: he'd bought Fanny a surprise present from Harrods pet department; could we go and collect it and join them for brunch?

We parked the Porsche on Pont Street, and walked to Harrods. To my horror the present turned out to be a bright green parrot in a large cage, and it was already squawking like mad at the thought of going anywhere. There was no way that the present would fit in the car, so I hailed a taxi and clambered in with it. On arrival at Claridge's, even though the cage was covered in wrapping paper, the bird started making an unholy racket, and the doormen were in fits of laughter. I telephoned the suite and Christopher told Fanny

to hide in the bathroom. Tim and I rang their bell, then entered their suite and placed the package in the centre of the dining table. Fanny emerged from the bathroom and was speechless! She adored the bird and immediately named him Claridge. He used to accompany them on holiday to the South of France, and travel around St Tropez sitting on her head. Claridge eventually died after about ten years, and a post mortem revealed he was an alcoholic – he had cirrhosis of the liver. He used to sit on our shoulders and swig Scotch, wine, vodka, anything . . .

For Christmas 1971 Tim and I had the idea of making a card in which I was a fairy sitting on his shoulders – he'd be dressed as a tree. But when we got to the costume hirers, I discovered that all the fairy outfits were for kids up to ten years old, and I couldn't get them on; and there were no tree costumes. Tim ended up hiring a troll outfit, and I settled for a vulture, complete with foam-rubber claws for my feet and large feathered wings. The result didn't look very seasonal, but was certainly a talking point.

We spent that Christmas in Cornwall at Patrick and Delia Heron's house, with Alex, Zandra, and Patrick's daughter Katharine, who had been in my year at college and was a really good friend. The weather was fantastic, cold with clear blue skies. When Zandra and I went for a walk along the narrow road down from Patrick's house, outside Zennor, west towards the clifftops at Gurnard's Head on Christmas Day we nearly caused a few crashes. Her hair was dyed blue and fastened in a roll on top of her forehead. She had bright pink splotches of rouge on her cheeks, and sooty black eye make-up, and sported a long rabbit-fur coat striped in rainbow colours from navy to red to cream. I wore a green fur jacket, a rainbow-coloured shawl made by my Welsh granny and a red felt

hat from under which my pink streaked hair stuck out in tufts. There was no danger of mistaking us for anyone else!

Early in January 1972 Tim and I at last found our new home, in a part of London that we could just about afford – in Narrow Street, Limehouse, the same house where Fred Grunfeld had once rented a flat. Mrs Woodward Fisher, the eccentric owner of the property, was selling it for £25,000. In the 1970s Limehouse wasn't gentrified at all. No one would give us a mortgage for such an old building directly on the water in such an unfashionable part of London, and in desperation I went down to Lewisham to visit Mrs WF in her control room on the ground floor of a vast Edwardian villa, hoping to butter her up and get a reduction in the price. She greeted me wearing her customary monocle and pin-striped man's suit, with a parrot on one shoulder, and continued barking instructions through a two-way radio set to her employees running her fleet of barges and tugs on the Thames. Dorothea (as I was instructed to call her) and I hit it off, and she gave us another month to find some financing.

In the end we got a mortgage from the Co-op for

£14,000, Tim's father lent us £7,000, and we managed to scrimp together the balance. The house was pretty run down: the ground floor had been a barge-repair yard, the first floor was a one room studio, and the top floor another one-room flat and a bathroom. But it faced south, with balconies over the water, with sun all day and the best view of the Thames in London, on the outside of a giant curve of water. We looked upstream to Wapping and Tower Bridge and downstream to the Isle of Dogs. At the end of our short terrace was the historic pub the Grapes, and Dr David Owen and his literary agent wife,

Deborah, lived a few doors along, as did television documentary maker Jenny Barraclough and her husband, who was a doctor. Although the houses were somewhat isolated, the shops were rubbish and the local eating opportunities confined to a couple of Chinese cafés, the atmosphere of the area, with its shimmering light and constantly changing water, was fantastic.

The day of our move was a disaster, because Chelsea were playing at home at Stamford Bridge and there was nowhere to park outside our flat. We'd hired a van and put all our belongings in black plastic rubbish bags, which we dragged down the stone stairs from the fourth floor. Helped by Zandra, Alex and a couple of other friends, we loaded the van during the match, and then made our way over to E14. We'd thrown a massive 'Goodbye to Chelsea' party the night before (the invites featured a picture of Tim, me and Tony Curtis) and I was definitely feeling the worse for wear. Imagine my horror when we eventually offloaded all these black garbage bags into the ground floor of 90 Narrow Street to discover we'd transported all the rubbish from every flat in our building!

We camped in the house for about six months, trying

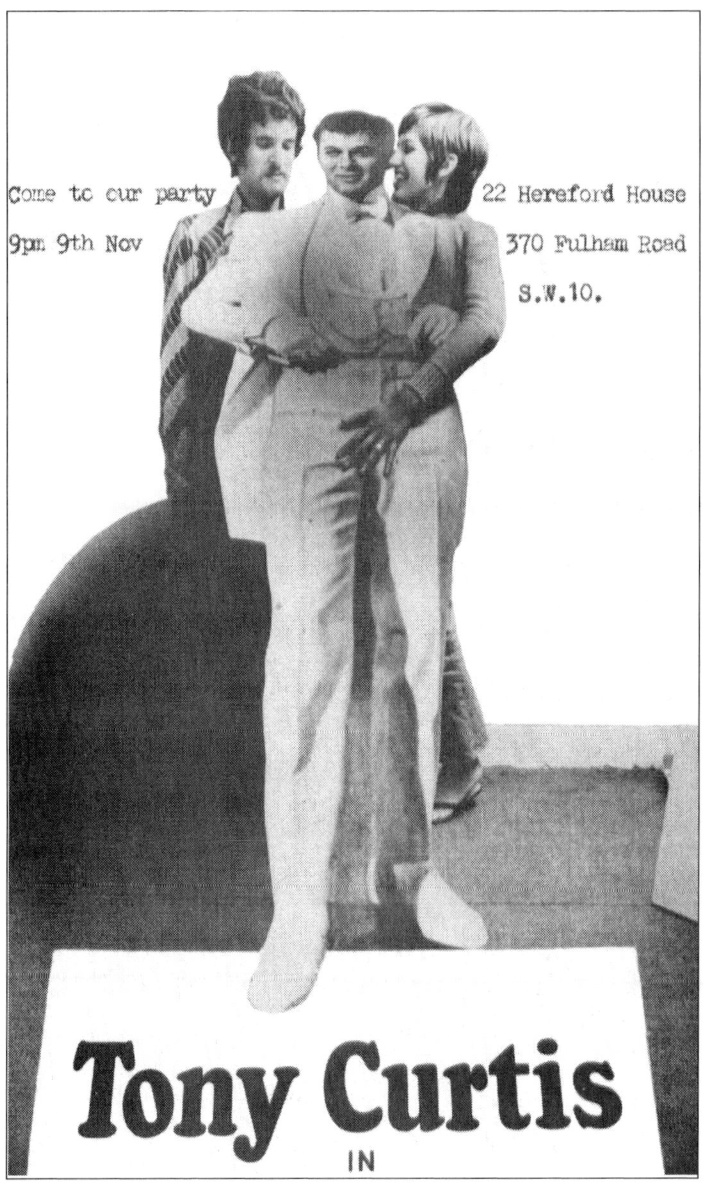
Come to our party
9pm 9th Nov
22 Hereford House
370 Fulham Road
S.W.10.
Tony Curtis
IN

to work out how to make it into a home on very little money. Eventually the architect Max Clendinning (in whose elegant Islington house I'd been photographed modelling white clothes for *Petticoat* three years before) designed our kitchen, with custom-made hardwood cabinets lacquered pillar-box red, and white tiled surfaces and floor. We left the 60-foot-long living room alone, painting the bare brick walls white, and polishing the wooden floor. The first-floor loo became a laundry room.

On the second floor, Tim built a unit which held loud-speakers and our mattress – it had a carpeted headboard and a wide shelf round it for lounging on and snacking in bed. Sebastian Conran had just left college, and he built us black lacquered cupboards and shelves. We covered the wall facing the river with beautiful hand-printed silver wallpaper designed by Zandra. On the other side of the wall, Tim built a dressing room, which we painted black, and we made a bathroom filled with 1930s glass panels salvaged from old shops. One of the best pieces of mirror was covered in sandblasted fish and waves and had come from a chip shop down the road from my childhood home in Fulham. All those hours spent scouring fleamarket stalls in Paris, Edgware Road and Notting Hill Gate for art deco had really paid off. The cutout of Tony Curtis was given pride of place in the living room. Now we had to adjust to the sound of river sirens and the creaking of the barges moored four deep outside our windows. It was so romantic.

Limehouse wasn't near any tube stations, and, as I couldn't drive, I tried a variety of ways to get to work at the *Evening Standard*. I'd get the bus on Commercial Road, or badger Tim to give me a lift to Tower Hill tube, at the other end of the bleak stretch of road called the Highway, or, if I was late, summon a local minicab. I even tried cycling to work – and the features editor turned it into a story!

There were no shops nearby, and soon I was busy ordering groceries to be delivered from Harrods on the days when my cleaning lady was in the house. On Sundays we'd drive up the Highway to Cannon Street Road, in Whitechapel, and the last Jewish deli left in the area, run by a fat, genial man called Mr Rogg. It had rows of barrels and sawdust on the floor and his bulldog slumped in the corner, gloomily watching over the shop. We'd select home-cured cucumbers, locally smoked salmon from

Bethnal Green, sourdough bread and bagels, chopped liver and pickled herrings, and invite friends over for a huge brunch.

When we moved in, Dan Farson, journalist, drinker and wit, lived next door to us at No 92, but he soon left to run a pub on the Isle of Dogs and our new neighbours were an eccentric elderly Royal Academician called Edward (Teddy) Wolfe and his boyfriend, a loquacious middle-aged Irishman called Jim O'Connor. Teddy was born in South Africa, and came to Britain as a teenager. He was close friends with the surviving members of the Bloomsbury group of artists, Duncan Grant in particular.

Teddy's house was completely unlike ours: a warren of small spaces, hung with his still lifes of flowers and fruit. His studio was a large room over the boatyard next door, full of junk furniture and unfinished canvases. He and Jim were always short of money, but the most hospitable people you could imagine, and soon we were eating with them several times a week. One Saturday a taciturn old man appeared clad entirely in black leather, with a young male ballet dancer in tow – it was Duncan Grant, rather grandly paying a visit.

Tim and I were out most evenings, at art gallery private views, the cinema and theatre, and I always loved arriving home to Narrow Street and falling asleep to the sound of the river. Doug Hayward was a friend of Christopher Ward, and had recently split up with his wife – he seemed to be living in hotel rooms near his shop. Among his closest friends were Michael Parkinson and his wife, Mary, and the journalist and lyricist Herbie Kretzmer (he wrote 'She' for Charles Aznavour as well as the lyrics to *Les Misérables*). One of the reasons I felt so at ease with Doug was his working-class background, which he made a complete virtue. At the *Daily Mail* the journalists I'd worked with like Lynda Lee-Potter had 'nice' middle-class accents, and Suzy Menkes, on the *Standard*, had been to Cambridge and certainly had a posh voice, as did most of the people who were successful in the media, from radio, to print to television. Through film stars like Michael Caine and Terence Stamp and photographers like David Bailey, it was no longer considered a disadvantage to sound working-class – in fact being a cockney, as long as you weren't running anything serious like a bank or a big business, was highly fashionable. Doug had been born in Hayes, west London, and briefly served in the navy. He'd done his tailoring apprenticeship at Bailey and Wetherall in Savile Row, but was not allowed to graduate to become a cutter because of his working-class accent. Even tailoring operated on a strict class system in those days.

After working in partnership in Fulham at Major Hayward he steadily built up his own clientele and eventually opened a shop on Mount Street, round the corner from the Connaught and Claridge's (handy for visiting American film stars) and nowhere near that bastion of the tailoring establishment Savile Row. Soon Doug had Michael Caine as a client – and even got an on-screen credit for dressing him in *The Italian Job*. He made suits for Terence Stamp, the upper-class photographer Patrick Lichfield and his cockney rival Terence Donovan. Another photographer, Terry O'Neill, was soon a customer, as well as Roger Moore (Doug did loads of clothes for the Bond movies), Rex Harrison and Vidal Sassoon. In short, Doug's shop was quite simply the most fashionable and agreeable place to hang out, drink a cup of tea, buy a tie or choose a sweater.

Doug was 100 per cent discreet, never grassing on any of his male mates who might be having affairs. He was definitely a man's man, and was an assiduous networker before the term was even contemplated. His affability meant that he could lunch with local landlord Mark Birley, the owner of Annabel's (the snootiest private nightclub in town), or a scruffy David Bailey. Bianca Jagger had been dating the boss of a French record label when she arrived in London looking for modelling work. She met Michael Caine in Doug's shop, and they had a brief affair, before he dumped her – and her next relationship was with Mick Jagger, who went on to become her first husband.

Doug was totally uninterested in high fashion – he had his own distinctive and flattering way of cutting suits, his casual style, and that was it. Consequently he was effortless company, just as happy to sit in a pub as to lunch with Lord Lichfield or Harry Hambleden, whose family were major shareholders in W. H. Smith and on whose Berkshire estate near the Thames Doug eventually rented a farmhouse for weekends. When he visited us in Limehouse one Sunday, we set out exploring the local pubs, and discovered that the Queen's Head, a very basic place by a block of council flats at the end of the Highway, had a Billy Fury impersonator singing at Sunday lunchtimes. Soon Parkie, Doug and I would often drop in, much to the astonishment of the regulars, and when it was chucking-out time, we'd head off to lunch at the White Elephant on the river in Pimlico.

Another great friend of Doug was the Jamaican businessman and advertising executive John Pringle, whose family had founded the Roundhill resort outside Montego Bay, where everyone from Jackie Kennedy to Princess Margaret and Ava Gardner had stayed. Pringle was one of the biggest eaters I'd ever met – we'd go round to his flat in Rutland Gate on a Sunday evening for a Jamaican feast cooked by his housekeeper, Blanche, and after curried goat, jerk chicken, rice and peas and rotis we'd have to lie on the floor to get over the carbohydrate overload! Soon Doug and his friends decided to open their own dining club just off Bond Street and called it Burkes, because it was about and for everyone who wasn't in *Burke's Peerage*, the old establishment.

Swinging London had a new aristocracy and it was nothing to do with your dad's bloodline and everything to do with what you did for a living and who you knew – it was full of advertising executives like Frank Lowe and Maurice Saatchi, film directors like John 'Point Blank' Boorman and visiting designers like Ralph Lauren. Burkes served basic nursery food – steaks, fish cakes, shepherd's pie and roasts (it was the prototype for the Ivy in many ways) – and the elegant dining room was lined with colourful still life paintings by Stanley Kubrick's wife, Christianne. Doug ate there every single weekday, drinking a large Scotch, smoking and holding court. As my job as a fashion writer took me to the West End to fashion showrooms, shops and photographers' studios, I joined him once or twice a week, always sitting at his regular table. That's how I met Terry Stamp (always on a weird diet, even then – once I remember he was only eating avocados for some reason) and Joan Collins, then about to relaunch her acting career.

The physical side of my relationship with Doug fizzled out, but we stayed very good friends. He made me a beautiful grey flannel trouser suit as well as an elegant denim-blue linen tailored jacket. I paid the earth for him to design me a double cashmere, floor-length, single-breasted, black overcoat with a velvet collar – exactly like a man's – and I still wear it today.

One day a couple of years later Doug called me up and asked me to go to Saturday lunch in Chelsea at La Famiglia to meet his new 'bird'. I knew it must be serious. She was called Lucy, a very glamorous American with short jet-black hair and loads of style. Doug's idea of taking this well-bred woman on a hot date was to drag her off to watch the football at Chelsea – somehow she survived the experience, and they were together for years. She replaced Doug as one of my very best friends until her death a few years ago.

Chapter 5

By the end of 1972 I was tiring of writing for the *Evening Standard*. It was a hell of a lot of work – we had to fill an eight-page fashion colour supplement on Mondays, as well as producing stories nearly every day in the paper, and I wrote a column for the Saturday edition, too. Fashion seemed increasingly irrelevant – at least in terms of my career – and there was only so much I could write about hemlines, hot pants and satin blazers. I felt that, with a few exceptions, designers were treading water, and the direction of fashion was being driven by ordinary people on the street, rather than via the whims of a few couturiers. I was desperate to broaden my horizons and get fresh inspiration and new things to write about.

That meant visiting America, and now the time seemed right. At peace talks in Paris, on 23 January 1973, the USA and Vietnam had signed an official ceasefire; since that 1968 anti-war demonstration in Grosvenor Square, over 56,000 American troops had died and over 270,000 had been wounded. There was a strange atmosphere in London. It seemed as if a backlash had begun against everything the Stones and David Bowie represented, from bisexuality to glam rock to drugs. Over the past few months Lord Longford had begun his campaign against pornography – he'd written to me and I went to the House of Lords and had lunch with him. He was a charming man, if somewhat eccentric and other-worldly. I thoroughly disagreed with everything he and his major ally, Mary Whitehouse (who ran a pressure group called the National Viewers and Listeners Association), were trying to achieve – it seemed like a futile attempt to turn back the clock. I went to the cocktail party at the Waldorf Hotel in the Aldwych, to launch the publication of Lord Longford's pornography report, and was very entertained to see him accosted by Xaviera Hollander, a feisty Dutch girl who had just written her memoirs, entitled *The Happy Hooker*.

In February 1973 I handed in three months' notice to the editor of the *Evening Standard*, Charles Wintour. He was a formidable character, dour in the extreme, but had been a big supporter of mine throughout my stint there. He coughed up an impressive pay rise of £35 a week straight away to cover all the extra work I'd been doing, but he reluctantly had to accept I would still be leaving, because it was the subject matter rather than money which was the problem.

The Institute of Contemporary Arts in the Mall was looking at ways of trying to attract a wider audience into the gallery, and I came up with 'The Body Show'. On a limited budget, and after months of planning, the big gallery was transformed into a hall of mirrors, over which floated a giant pink inflatable woman with long strands of yellow plastic hair, designed by Piers Gough. For 50p visitors bought an hour of fun: free facials, manicures, pedicures and snapshots. We managed to persuade manufacturers like Scholl, Miners, Revlon, Cutex, Fabergé, Rochas and Mary Quant to supply not only free makeup but the people to apply it, too. It was a huge success, as were the rag books designed by Brian Clark, with all the credits printed on them and with pink flannel covers to wipe your face clean.

On the Sunday evening a boxing ring was erected and the lecturer and designer Gordon Deighton staged a fashion show with top models, wrestlers and boxers. It was absolutely sold out – everyone liked the combination of clothes by artists, students and commercial designers. Allen Jones had some extremely erotic underwear specially made by Mary Quant, there were some really weird clothes as food designed by fashion students, and Zandra Rhodes and Ossie Clark made stuff especially for

the event. There were ethnological one-off clothes in cotton and wool by Nanni Strada from Milan, and body sculpture by Emmy van Leeersum and Gris Bakker from the Netherlands. Manolo Blahnik designed the shoes and Leonard the hair – we really put together a top team. I went on television to talk about the event and some of the pieces were shown on BBC2's *Late Night Line-Up*. After the show we held a party with fire eaters and a disco – I don't think the ICA had ever seen anything like it.

Joan Littlewood called me up – she was running the Theatre Royal at Stratford East, where she'd had a huge success with *Oh What a Lovely War*, which had been turned from a musical into a film (directed by Richard Attenborough). I met Joan and her manager, Gerry Raffles, and we talked about how to change 'The Body Show' so it would work in a Victorian theatre with a proscenium arch in a working-class area in the heart of the East End rather than in an art gallery just down the road from Buckingham Palace. She persuaded the actors Victor Spinetti and George Sewell (both regulars in her shows) to take part, and I managed to get enough free cosmetics and staff to fill the bar and give members of the audience free make-overs before the show. Victor would play a *Cabaret*-style camp Master of Ceremonies and George (known to everyone as Chuck) would be his usual gangster type.

We used the same models as at the ICA and the same director. Once again Leonard did the models' hair and Barbara Daly their makeup – by now they were both at the very top of their game, working with people like Twiggy and on movies like Stanley Kubrick's *Barry Lyndon*, so it was a real coup to get them for free on a Sunday night in the depths of east London. Joan was completely thrilled, and the show was a sell-out – almost six hundred tickets were snapped up. The audience loved the bodybuilders and the fire-eaters, and screamed with delight during the wrestling, and the evening went really well. Even so, Joan sent me a little postcard a few days later, noting that, although the place had been packed, we'd only broken even, and adding, 'All of which proves what I know only too well, that this old dump cannot make a profit, even with a smash! It was a great night, please use this place again . . .'

My salary on the *Standard* was increased again in April, to £3,975 a year, but by then I had already gone to the *Observer Colour Magazine* and extracted a commission to write three stories from the USA, accompanied by Tim's photographs. I also agreed to write some opinion pieces for Audrey Slaughter's new glossy magazine, *Over 21* – they had run a very positive feature about me the previous summer, and Audrey had given me my first break on *Petticoat* back in 1969.

Lord Longford's anti-pornography campaign had taken a bit of a knock when the film *Last Tango in Paris* opened in London in 1972. I rushed to see it, and was rather disappointed – it was one long bonk, but you had to suspend belief to accept that the character played by the extremely nubile young actress Maria Schneider would have found the ageing and distinctly podgy Marlon Brando a sex god . . . It seemed rather stagey, to say the least. The anti-smut lobby then made a huge fuss over a documentary David Bailey had shot about Andy Warhol for commercial television, and there was legal action to try and prevent it being shown on the grounds of depravity! Bailey responded by publishing a transcript of the documentary as a large-format book, complete with stills, which sold really well. Eventually the film was televised at the end of March 1973, and no one could understand what all the fuss had been about. Mary

Whitehouse and Lord Longford's Petition for Public Decency (with 1,350,000 signatures) was presented to the prime minister, Ted Heath. I prayed he'd chuck it straight in the bin.

Tim and I had planned our US trip carefully to make our money go as far as possible. We decided to rent out the house in Narrow Street while we were away, buy a car in New York, where we'd stay with our friend Stephen Naab, and drive all the way across America to Los Angeles, where we'd made plans to stay in an artist's studio on the beach in Venice for a month, and then rent a house behind Tower Records on Sunset Strip for another few weeks – I couldn't wait! We left London on a Saturday at the end of April, with massive suitcases stuffed with clothes, cameras and a typewriter. We touched down at eight in the evening in New York and it was a warm night. I was exhausted by the time we got through the queues in immigration, collected all our luggage and finally arrived at Stephen's apartment, just off Central Park on West 83rd Street.

We rang the bell, but there was no answer. We tried again and again. Eventually we rang the bell marked 'Super' and were buzzed inside after we said we were looking for Stephen in apartment 6A. The other tenants on his floor weren't of much help. 'You'll be lucky,' said one couple, when I asked if they had any idea where he was. 'He's often out all night – God knows what he gets up to . . .'

The door was wide open, but there was no one at home. In the bathroom a giant bullwhip hung from the shower head and towels were all over the floor. The kitchen was a mess, full of unwashed glasses. In the living room the lights were on, as if the occupant had just popped out to get some cigarettes or a beer. My first trip to America wasn't exactly starting in the way that I'd expected.

Tim and I had met Stephen a year or so before through Zandra Rhodes. He'd appeared one Christmas, a buddy of her Texan pal the designer Richard Holley, and had entertained us all with his party tricks and outrageous behaviour. Our friend Moya Bowler invited him to a festive dinner in Notting Hill, and when he found the conversation was not to his liking, he decided to liven up the evening by eating several of the glass balls on the Christmas tree. Moya burst into tears; Stephen then ate a wine glass. Moya started beating him on the chest, to no avail. He was fearless and a massive drinker, the complete party animal.

A thick-set man in his late 30s, Stephen had met Richard at college in New York, where they'd studied design. He worked intermittently as an interior designer, relying on a few very rich elderly Jewish ladies to keep him in Tiffany silver and crystal. Stephen soon came to London regularly, and on one occasion I'd been photographed dancing in a nightclub with him at someone's birthday party. I was wearing a very beautiful embroidered black and white silk Zandra Rhodes blouse and large white pearls. Stephen was almost naked. He'd decided the party needed pepping up a bit, so he'd taken most of his clothes off. The picture (with a strategically placed blob) appeared a couple of days later in a newspaper gossip column. Stephen had been thrilled, but I'd had my leg pulled mercilessly at work.

His non-appearance now was the last straw. It was too late to phone anyone in London to see if they'd heard from him. I wasn't sure what to do, and going out to dinner was out of the question because we had no keys to get back in. Tim walked down to the grocery store at the end of the street to get some beers and stuff for supper,

and I collapsed on the bed in what I guessed was the spare bedroom.

After a few drinks and a couple of sandwiches, I had a shower – couldn't find any towels so I used my T-shirt – and fell into a fitful sleep, waking up every couple of hours because of imagined sounds, unused to my new surroundings. We had decided to lock the front door – surely Stephen would have taken his key with him? I finally woke up properly at 6 a.m., wrapped myself in a sheet and tiptoed down the corridor. The place was still completely empty. When Tim woke, at around eight, we were mystified – this was getting beyond a joke. We made some coffee and I started to get to grips with cleaning the kitchen. I'd already tidied up the living room, plumped the cushions on the large sofas, dusted the coffee-table tops and removed the overflowing ashtrays and dirty glasses. I was moaning like hell – I hadn't come all this way to morph into a fucking cleaning lady – when there was a ring on the buzzer.

Tim opened the front door and there was Stephen, naked except for a horrible brown felt blanket tied round his thickening middle like a very stylish roman toga. Who could still be angry with this irrepressible madman? He was incorrigible.

Over breakfast he explained that the day before he'd had a few drinks with a friend and decided to pop down to Central Park for a spot of last-minute cruising before we arrived. He'd been lurking behind some bushes when he'd got lucky. As he was rather drunk he'd decided to strip off in order to enter into the spirit of the orgy properly. Unfortunately the police suddenly appeared from nowhere, and he was handcuffed and arrested. In the confusion all his clothes – and his keys – were left behind in the park, and he'd spent a night in the cells, before appearing in court at nine that morning, charged with lewd behaviour. He'd been given a blanket to come home in, and had a cab waiting downstairs, which needed paying. Tim went and did the business while I sat open-mouthed.

There was no point whatsoever in trying to understand the way Stephen's mind worked. He could have been beaten up or robbed at the very least, but that never seemed to bother him. In fact, this had happened several times, but he still regularly cruised Central Park and brought strangers back to his flat. This was before Aids was around, and I suppose he thought the worst thing he might catch was VD. He'd got lucky the night before the arrest, hence the whip in the bathroom – I couldn't bear to think about what he'd got up to with it.

Stephen might have been strapped for funds, but he was a brilliant host. He had cupboards full of the finest crystal, Tiffany silver and beautiful dinner plates. He was an excellent cook, and would light his large brown-painted living room with masses of candles to produce the most seductive atmosphere. The trouble was, if he had just one drink too many, or if someone got on the wrong side of him, it could all degenerate into a screaming match – and his tongue was vicious, his put-downs unforgettable, generally resulting in the guest storming off or Stephen throwing them out.

During our week in residence he decided to host a dinner party for us – we supplied the funds for the food and wine – and inevitably it ended with one of his friends in tears, and Stephen storming off to the park. Next day, he had airbrushed the incident from his memory, and showered and smartened up to extricate some cash from one of his clients. We went to a party at the Museum of Modern Art, and Stephen managed to get us introduced to an astonishing little old lady who carried a diamond-encrusted walking stick. She was Mrs Gimbel, of the department store family, over 80 years old and bright as a button.

I spent the next couple of days exploring New York, with Stephen showing me the Village and pointing out the best boutiques, while Tim went out to New Jersey to buy a Volkswagen Beetle from an ad in the *New York Times*. Our epic journey was about to begin. Only two problems: the car had gears and I couldn't drive, so I'd have to be a passenger all the way from coast to coast. We hoped to get most of our money back by flogging the vehicle at the end of our trip before we returned to London.

Luckily, I had got my map-reading badge in the Girl Guides and we managed to get onto the right freeway out of the city without too much hassle. We'd left Stephen a present of some booze, and, amazingly, he was still speaking to us – we hadn't overstayed our welcome. He'd even phoned his brother Christopher in Washington and asked if we could stay with him for a night.

It was pouring with rain when we arrived and drove up to a smart detached house in the suburbs. Christopher was physically like Stephen, but there the resemblance ended – he had a good job as a lawyer or something to do with money (I can't remember now), and he was married with children. When he heard about our bizarre arrival at his brother's flat, he burst into laughter and said, 'Nothing would ever surprise me about Stephen!' We tried to drive around Washington and see the sights, but the rain was torrential. The Watergate hearings were about to begin, and we watched Nixon on television accepting responsibility but not taking the blame for the scandal, an astonishing moment. There was the feeling everywhere that momentous events were about to unfold and fresh revelations were imminent.

We left town next day in even worse rain and started driving through West Virginia. I thought the car was going to slide off the road in the floodwater, and started grizzling. When we stopped at a diner for brunch, there was silence as I walked through the door. The people inside were all fat, white and hostile. Of course in London our appearance was hardly the stuff of comment, and no one had batted an eyelid in New York. But here my yellow streaks, big white spectacle frames and tiny shorts and Tim's shoulder-length curly hair and moustache meant only one thing: we were left-wing hippies. I sat down at the counter and tried to order my breakfast with an audience hanging on my every word. I might as well have been speaking in Urdu for all they understood. The only Brits these kind of people had ever heard of were the Beatles and the Rolling Stones – over and over again during the next couple of weeks I was asked if Tim was a Beatle and if I knew Mick Jagger!

Luckily Tim had lived in the States for a couple of years and was well-versed in the ritual of ordering eggs sunny side up, over easy, and all that mindless ritual Americans apply to ordering stuff that barely qualifies as nourishing fare. Over the next week I was to eat nothing but fast food, and days went past without me seeing any kind of vegetable except a slice of tomato or a lifeless bit of iceberg lettuce. I took one tiny sip of Coca-Cola and loathed it. As for American coffee, it was weak, watery and sour. I was definitely going to have to stop being so choosy if I didn't want to starve. We decided to stay in roadside motels. They never cost more than thirty dollars for a huge room, usually with two double beds and acres of carpet which was often covered with dubious-looking stains. This was the trip where I perfected my shower-hat routine. I began to collect them and would pop one on each foot as instant slippers – there was no way my skin was touching those disgusting carpets, which reeked of cigarettes and French fries.

The worst place we stopped at was just outside Memphis, on Route 66 – it was a Sunday, and the diner was crammed to bursting. As I walked through the room to get to the ladies' toilet all conversation stopped. On my way back to our booth, I heard a repulsively obese white woman with her hair in rollers (covered by a headscarf) and wearing baggy Bermuda shorts say to her friends, 'Just take a look at that! Oh, lawdy, have you ever seen anything like it?' I fled to the car in tears – it was unlike me not to have a pithy put-down to hand, but after days on the road I felt like a fish out of water, miles from home. The best thing about the journey was the radio stations, and now we were in the deep south we had Johnny Cash and country and western from dawn till dusk.

Things improved after Dallas, when we skirted south towards the Mexican border – the music on the radio was captivating, and I loved the sound of the mariachi bands and their endless crooning of love songs, with all sorts of exuberant flourishes and repetitive choruses. It

was great for my Spanish – I could sing along as we cruised through the wide dusty prairie. El Paso was fabulous, teeming with people and the smells of taco stands – and the food was at last something I could really enjoy – huevos rancheros with beans for breakfast, tacos for lunch and chicken cooked in chocolate for dinner. I was in heaven after days of unappetising burgers and rubbery omelettes! El Paso was right off the tourist trail, full of dilapidated 1940s buildings, drive-ins painted with giant murals of cowboys and inviting dark bars. We stayed in a motel in the middle of nowhere, about ten miles out of town. The owner had a beautiful hand-tooled leather three-piece suite in reception, decorated with cattle horns. I had to stop myself buying it and shipping it back home! Next stop was a western outfitters, and we both bought cowboy boots and shirts – mine was red and white gingham and my boots dark green.

We eventually drove through the Nevada desert and onto the freeway into Los Angeles – I'd never been on a road with so many lanes and so many cars passing each other on both sides – it was pretty scary. We left the Santa Monica Freeway just before Ocean Drive, and turned south towards Venice. Our friends had the keys to the place we'd arranged to rent, a studio belonging to an artist called Chuck Arnoldi, just off the beach. It was in a former bakery on Brooks Avenue, and was a simple industrial box, with no side windows and a lot of locks on the front door. Further down the street was a mural covering the whole side of a dilapidated apartment building, showing the view in the opposite direction, which was pretty disconcerting.

Back in 1973 Venice was a run-down neighbourhood, with streets of small villas and an area of decaying blocked-up canals. The seafront boardwalk could be quite rough, with regular fights over drugs among the down-and-outs who hung out all day on the benches around the recreation area. But many artists had taken advantage of low rents to buy big industrial spaces, which they kept looking as low-key as possible on the outside in order not to attract attention. Leading artists like Larry Bell, Laddie Dill, Billy Al Bengston and Robert Graham all lived and worked within a couple of hundred yards of each other. We'd never met Chuck Arnoldi, but the others had exhibited in London at the Felicity Samuels Gallery on Cork Street and we'd got to know them through mutual friends.

Chuck obviously wasn't the scholarly type: apart from a few old issues of *National Geographic* there was no printed matter in the place at all! It was full of his large sculptures made from sticks, with an austere bedroom and bathroom, but it suited us perfectly. Later, when I went back to California the following year, he became one of my best friends there, but this time he was just an absent landlord. Billy Al lived round the corner in Mildred Avenue with his girlfriend, Penny Little – he owned the entire building, which he used as office, studio and living accommodation. Larry Bell was in Market Street, near Bob Graham.

The noise at night in Venice was astonishing – bongo drums would be going for hours, or searing electric guitars. I took the locals' advice and didn't wear any jewellery in case I got mugged by the junkies hanging out when I went to the supermarket. In between the drug houses and squats some villas were being extensively refurbished, with high, boarded fences erected round them to keep out the burglars. I loved the funky mixture of druggies, derelicts, musicians and street theatrics on the boardwalk. Then there were the bodybuilders from the gym round the corner, who loved to work out in the open-air weight-lifting area next to the paddle tennis courts. Down the boardwalk towards Santa Monica was a Jewish old people's home, and pairs of elderly ladies and gentlemen would be wheeled through this melting pot by nurses in uniform. On Sundays there were hundreds of tourists and sightseers and black kids would dance for money.

Soon, we were shopping at the local market and behaving like seasoned residents. We drove down to Tijuana to cross into Mexico for the Baja 500, the off-road race we planned to cover for the *Observer*. Nobody in the UK had ever heard of off-road racing, and few Californians had been to Baja – but to free spirits and adventurers it represented the last place to escape the rules and regulations of America. Baja was part of Mexico, a desolate and empty finger of land running south of the border, a hundred miles longer than Italy, with a thousand miles of Pacific coastline. The sport of off-roading had started in California about seven years earlier with the development of beach buggies and other recreational vehicles. Enthusiasts realised that these cars could be customised to compete over rough terrain in wilderness areas, and by 1973 there were thousands of followers and four big races a year, two of which were in Baja. When we went to Ensenada, the tiny fishing village at the northern end of the route, the paved road only extended a fraction of the distance down the peninsula – the rest was a series of rutted dusty tracks. The Baja 500 attracted a wide cross-section of racers, from house-wives to professional drivers like the Indianapolis champion Parnelli Jones in their customised cars – the actor Steve McQueen had tried it one year, and this time James Garner was giving it a go.

We arrived a couple of days before the race and had trouble finding a motel room – it was sweltering and the place was packed. Every parking space, from dried out river beds to building sites, was full of the most incredible cars and motorbikes I'd ever seen, sprouting roll bars, padding, giant exhausts and lurid paint jobs. The bars were packed with swarthy tough guys – and being plucky Brits, we really stood out, with our white skin and Limey accents. Soon, we were being bought margharitas and trying to stay sober enough to work out how two people, one of whom couldn't drive, could cover a race 610 miles long. Bernice, aged 49, was racing a VW with her son Dan 'just for fun', while Bobby Ferro, aged 24, who had won the previous two years running and was considered a 'real hot dog', was taking everything very seriously indeed. Parnelli Jones, who had the most expensive car, a monster sponsored by Olympia Beer and Ford, sported a crew cut combed over a receding hairline, and his age wasn't listed in the programme. But he had arms like bridge supports, and added a touch of glamour to the proceedings by keeping his car firmly under wraps until the big day, and flying in by helicopter.

The night before the race we attended a hilarious drivers' meeting in the village hall – most of it was spent establishing the exact course, which would be over virgin desert and rarely used dirt tracks, marked with pink fluorescent ribbons. Checkpoints would be 100 miles apart, so if there were crashes the drivers would be on their own. Farmers would have to be compensated for any livestock killed.

Race day was hot and humid. Tim had hitched a lift out of town at 4.30 a.m. to set up his cameras by a spectacular bend fringed with giant 'boojum' trees in the desert. I watched as the drivers left via the main street, cheered on by a crowd of around 1,000 fans, including a bunch of Mexican sailors wearing jackets covered in red pom-poms. The bike riders left first, and would have to negotiate through the hot central desert in the middle of the day. One rider managed to break his wrist only 300 yards down the road when he collided with an over-zealous traffic cop!

As the day went on, stories filtered back. One man broke his fingers when his car overturned in the desert –

the dust from the car in front made it impossible to see – and he simply made a rough and ready splint out of wood, strapped his arm to it, got back in the car and carried on. A bike rider was knocked out when he hit a tree. When he regained consciousness and got back on his bike, he went ten miles in the wrong direction before he realised his mistake. When it was dark Parnelli Jones streaked back into town in record time in just under twelve and a half hours, a full hour ahead of anyone else. By then I was completely drunk and the backs of my knees were red and raw with sunburn – it was the only place I'd forgotten to slather with lotion. Tim reappeared, caked white with dust from the desert, looking like a Martian, completely goggle-eyed. We spent the evening regaling each other with stories of what we'd seen and heard, and lapped up the crazy atmosphere as riders continued to arrive back right through the night, looking like survivors from a war zone. We would never forget the day we 'did it in the dirt', and it was the start of many trips down to Baja over the next couple of years.

Our next story was about another sport which hadn't taken off in the UK at all, and that was hang-gliding. I'd read a story in an American sports magazine about these fanatical madmen who built giant kites they attached themselves to and then jumped off cliffs, floating for miles completely unaided by an engine. One Sunday morning we drove down south again, this time near San Diego. Somehow I wasn't surprised that southern California should be the spawning ground for all these extreme activities. We turned inland and drove through a range of mountains, and then up a winding road to a series of grassy peaks where a hang-gliding championship was being held. It looked absolutely spectacular, the clear blue sky setting off the bright colours of the hang-gliders and the crash helmets worn by their pilots. It all seemed to be a matter of timing, finding the perfect breeze, and then the competitor ran towards the sheer drop and launched himself into the air. My heart stopped – I thought I was going to be sick – but they all immediately glided effortlessly over the valley, using the horizontal bar to guide and steer their machine.

Our third story for the *Observer* magazine was about the notorious maximum-security prison Alcatraz, in San Francisco Bay. I had found out that it was to be opened up as a National Park, and had written to the authorities asking permission to go and write about it. It had been occupied by the American Indians (as Native Americans were then known) from 1969 to 1971, protesting at their position as the least privileged group of people in America. There had been 600 people living on the island at the height of the occupation, and they survived a coastguard blockade and threats of removal by force. Eventually, they left of their own accord, thoroughly disillusioned. The last prison inmates had been moved out in 1963 – over the years they had included Al Capone, Floyd Hamilton of the Bonnie and Clyde gang and Robert 'Birdman' Stroud. In 1966 the derelict prison had been used as a setting for John Boorman's film *Point Blank*, starring Lee Marvin. There had been endless deliberations about what to do with the place – suggestions ranged from a nudist colony to a space-age museum to a giant Statue of Liberty. In the end the Golden Gate National Recreational Park authorities had decided to open it up to small groups of sightseers, with an hourly ferry service over the choppy waters of the bay connecting it with the waterfront tourist area, and Tim and I were the first journalists they allowed to see it before it opened to the public.

We drove north up the scenic coastal route from Los

Angeles in our trusty VW, passing through Santa Barbara and the rocky coastline of Big Sur and Monterey to San Francisco, and decided to stay in a motel in Berkeley, the scene of bitter student riots in the 1960s. The Watergate hearings were droning away on television in the background of every bar and restaurant. We sat mesmerised for hours in our hotel room, watching President Nixon give evidence – it all added to the general feeling of unreality.

I could see Alcatraz from every hilltop in San Francisco, but I wasn't prepared for the interior of the jail itself. The cell block had been built free-standing inside a large concrete structure, and the prisoners looked through their bars at bare walls. Windows were small, for ventilation only – anyone incarcerated would have been able to hear the crashing waves, the howling wind and squarking seagulls, but all they would have seen was wall. Not a scrap of sky – I nearly cried. At least 25 of them had tried to escape, five of whom were shot dead. No one is known to have survived the swim to the shore, although two men tunnelled their way out with sharpened spoons in 1962 and were never found. All that remained of the Indians' occupation was a disintegrating parcel from a well-wisher, which contained several rotting pairs of high-heeled shoes and handbags and had been chucked on the floor in disgust. Before they left, the Indians had sprayed a red eagle over the entrance to the main block and the names of Nixon, Reagan, Lyndon Johnson and Spiro T. Agnew over the doors of individual cells. Wishful thinking.

Soon it was time for us to head back to the UK. Tim managed to sell our car – we only lost a couple of hundred dollars on the purchase price, so it had been a good investment. We decided to fly straight back to London from Los Angeles and get our stories to the *Observer*. I really didn't want to leave Los Angeles as we had made so many close friends there, from artists like Ed Ruscha, Larry Bell and Billy Al Bengston to architects like Frank Gehry and art collectors like Joan and Jack Quinn – he was lawyer to most of the leading artists in town. Robin and Jessie French's old ranch house high above Coldwater Canyon was another hangout for this group. Robin was an English agent and promoter, and Jessie a wonderfully eccentric naive painter.

Tim and I decided to revisit Baja California one last time. We had fallen in love with the vast emptiness of the landscapes, the tall 'boojum' trees, the unspoilt miles of beaches and the hundreds of miles of dirt roads. One weekend a bunch of us drove down to the tiny coastal village of San Felipe on the Sea of Cortez, and stayed in a basic motel right on the beach. That night we had a taco-eating competition – and I managed to eat twelve, washed down with margharitas and Tecate beer. The sea was turquoise blue and totally clear. The others drove motorbikes and jeeps along the beach, and I collected driftwood while they fished and collected oysters off the rocks.

We decided to take on a final commission for the *Telegraph* colour magazine about the amazing houses that were being built in the very south, at Las Cruces, over the headland from the town of La Paz. The road down was extremely potholed, with long dirt sections, and petrol stations were few and far between. The thousand kilometres of Baja was mostly desert wilderness, with a few fishing villages and coastal lagoons where whale watchers congregated. We hitched a lift on a brand-new Cessna small plane to our hotel at the resort of Cabo San Lucas, at its very tip – in those days a small cluster of fishermen's houses with a handful of holiday villas and just a couple of newly built hotels in which to stay. On arrival we manage to persuade the owner of the plane to lend us it and the pilot for a day so that we could fly up to the hamlet of Las Cruces, where Bing Crosby and Desi Arnaz had spectacular houses. The community lay just over the mountains from La Paz, the main town at the southern end of the peninsula, but the millionaire home-owners had decided to dynamite the road to their properties, ensuring total privacy as now they were accessible only by boat or plane.

Desi Arnaz had been charming to us when we drove down to meet him in San Diego to arrange this trip. His villa at Las Cruces was extremely eccentric. Once he'd owned RKO Studios, where *Gone with the Wind* had been made decades earlier. When it came to furnishing his house, Desi simply raided the props store! In the living room was a huge mirror from one of the mansions in *Gone with the Wind*, and on the terrace outside the living room the saddle from *Destry Rides Again*. Next to the saddle was an ancient pool table from another Western – barely protected from the elements by a wide canopy. The swimming pool was guitar-shaped, and at its end was a fake Grecian folly. Bing Crosby's house, by comparison, was much more conventional. But we were really pleased with Desi's place, and we knew we'd be able to sell the story over and over again, making a good income.

Around five in the afternoon we decided it was time to leave, before sunset. We'd landed on a dirt track nearby and we were soon taxiing down it and climbing up over the mountains and heading back south to Cabo San Lucas. The pilot talked to air traffic control at La Paz and then to the owner of the plane, giving our arrival time. But when we reached the sandy landing strip at Cabo, there was a problem: the plane's nose-wheel was stuck inside the fuselage and would not drop down and lock into position for landing. The other two wheels (one in each wing) were fine, but without the third wheel to steady the plane there was a real possibility that the plane would flip over on landing and break up, or at the very least buckle and damage the wings – which is where the fuel was stored.

My stomach started churning. Normally I was quite relaxed about small planes. We'd used them before in Baja and I was accustomed to the way they'd suddenly drop 50 feet when they encountered pockets of hot air over the desert. But this was different. Tim and I looked at each other and froze. 'Don't worry,' said Chuck, the pilot. 'Tighten your seatbelts – I'm going to try a few loops and try to shake the darned thing out.' For the next 20 minutes we climbed vertically into the azure of the sky – and then jerked downwards, heading straight for the shark-infested turquoise sea below. We straightened out at the last minute, and repeated the loop. After four attempts I was glad I hadn't eaten much for lunch. Food might be ready to leave my stomach, but there was no way that bloody wheel was going to drop out of its casing inside the nose of the plane.

Next, a row ensued over the radio between the pilot and the plane's owner. The owner was most unhappy that his brand-new baby might get scratched on landing. He couldn't have cared less about us – it seemed to me as if he was far less bothered about our lives than about the paintwork on his bloody Cessna, and there was a lot of nitpicking about whether the plane was still under warranty. We flew back to La Paz as the light started to fade, and then out to sea for 30 minutes to use up as much fuel as possible. Tim and I were silent. I asked him for a pen and a bit of paper – he handed me a Kodak film carton, which was all he had. I tore it into two and wrote on one half, 'I love you,' and handed it to him. He smiled and tucked it in his pocket. On the other half I wrote my will – but there was no space, so I just wrote, 'In the event of my death I leave everything to Tim Street-Porter,' and signed it, stuffing it in my shorts pocket. Of course, if we crashed and there was a big fire, the note and I would both go up in smoke, but just doing a small thing like writing a sentence or two made me a little calmer.

Finally, after endless discussions with the airport authorities at La Paz airport – only one tarmac runway and a small building with a control tower – we were ready to land. Tim was told to get out of his seat and cram himself on the floor behind it in the tail, to act as ballast, I shifted to the centre of the two seats. Meanwhile, the pilot had decided to switch the engine off and glide in, landing in the dirt at the side of the runway. When the plane stopped we would have to open the door when the engine cut out. Gracefully the Cessna glided down, and with a huge bump the two rear wheels hit the dirt. The aircraft shuddered violently and tipped right up, the nose embedding itself in the soil. We clambered out and slid down the wings, shaking, into the arms of Mexican paramedics, then were bundled into a lorry with a red and white cross on the side – what passed for an ambulance in La Paz – and were driven at high speed back to the terminal.

There we hugged the pilot, each other, even the swarthy air traffic controller, who was very unimpressed with our crash. The walls of his office were covered with pictures of wrecked planes – he explained he liked to photograph them as a hobby. When engineers had checked there was no leaking fuel, we walked back to the Cessna, stuck in the ground like a pitchfork. Tim retrieved his camera bags, and the air traffic controller took one snap of our wreck – I doubted whether it would make his hall of fame.

After several cups of coffee, we sat through a gruelling two-hour taxi ride back to Cabo and our hotel, which was down a narrow, winding road full of ruts and potholes. It was pitch dark, and every now and then our driver had to swerve to avoid cars coming the other way with either no lights or one light. Animals kept making dashes for freedom across our path – rabbits and small mammals. Eventually we arrived back at the hotel, where we left the pilot to make his peace with the plane's owner. They had stopped serving dinner, so we just had a couple of beers and regaled everyone in the bar with our adventure before falling into bed. I dreamed of plane crashes for months afterwards, reliving that awful two hours in the air. I never found out what Tim did with the scrap of paper I'd given him, and just as mysteriously I never found my Kodak packet last Will and Testament.

Back in Los Angeles we decided to head straight home rather than risk another visit to Stephen. We hoped he wouldn't be offended, but the truth is he probably didn't even notice. I phoned and chatted to him – he planned to visit London as soon as he could raise the money. Luckily, he didn't ask if he could stay at our house, probably because Limehouse wasn't convenient enough for cruising. He preferred to stay with Moya Bowler or Zandra Rhodes in Notting Hill Gate because he adored Holland Park – and it wasn't because of the plants or dogs!

Back in London, we caught the Underground to Tower Hill, as it would have cost a fortune to get to E14 in a cab. I'd tried ringing our house before we left California, and tried again at Heathrow. No answer. We'd rented it to an art dealer who worked in Bond Street, and who had just split up with his wife. His mother was a friend of Teddy Wolfe, our next-door neighbour; they had known each other from their childhood in South Africa. Betty was a wonderfully entertaining woman and her son was charming in his own way. He'd been to public school and moved through the London art scene like a hot knife through butter, sucking up to rich patrons and collectors.

Perhaps we should have got some form of deposit from him before we let him stay, but it did seem a bit grasping and working-class. How wrong we were! Our house was a total wreck. The living room was filthy, the kitchen full of dirty plates, rotting food, half-full glasses and piles of rubbish. Upstairs in our bedroom the door onto our roof terrace had been smashed off its hinges, the carpet was covered in piles of nappies full of baby poo. The bath hadn't been cleaned for weeks and there were towels torn up to make more nappies. I felt sick. Our trip to the States had ended just as bizarrely as it had begun. Suddenly I realised that Stephen, for all his faults, was not a total shit, while our house-sitter with his public-school superiority, definitely was.

Chapter 6

A pile of envelopes lay scattered on my desk in the gloomy ground-floor offices of London Broadcasting in Gough Square, just off Fleet Street. Without exception they were small, blue, cream or brown, and addressed to me – using many versions of my name ranging from Jannette to Janit or Jeanete, all painstakingly inscribed with a biro or occasionally bashed out on an ageing typewriter. Not one envelope was made of that gorgeous thick white paper which meant a rather fabulous invite might be inside asking me to a party, night club opening or fashion show. No, these were the day's offerings from my new fan club. Except they weren't all fans.

*

Dear Jane Street-Porter,

Your voice!!!!

Your apparent personality

Your manner of interview

Personify and support everything that is LOW in Great Britain today.

I therefore hope that at the very least YOU are happy with the way you are earning your living.

Yours sincerely,

The usually silent majority

HAPPY NEW YEAR

I chucked it in the bin, but then retrieved it. I'd received so much hate mail over the past two and a half months that I was planning to recycle the most vitriolic efforts into a feature for a magazine – 'Waste not, want not' was definitely my slogan.

The man sitting behind the desk opposite me smirked. 'One of your usual admirers, old bean?'

'Fuck off, Paul, you piece of shit,' I retorted, and opened the newspaper to obliterate his fat, smug face from my line of vision.

*

When I returned to London from California at the end of July 1973, I was surprised to find how much I'd missed my home town. It was the longest time I'd ever been away, and I had begun to get severe withdrawal pangs. I'd loved the sun and laid-back atmosphere of Los Angeles, the Mexican food, the margharitas; I was fit from playing tennis every day and running along the beach. But I'd also sneaked off to the cinema (much to Tim's disgust) for little injections of nostalgia via Lindsay Anderson's new film *O Lucky Man!*, and a new thriller *The Day of the Jackal*, which starred a very glamorous James Fox. I'd been to Hollywood Boulevard to buy *Private Eye*, and tried to explain the concept of irony to Californians. Fat chance.

Back home, I knew within a day what it was I'd missed about London: the colour. Powdery, soft, velvety black. The colour of soot, the cinders on the track at the Speedway track, the colour of the road in Dean Street, the rain when I left a drinking club in the middle of a wet afternoon, the soil in the handkerchief sized gardens I saw from Underground train windows. The colour of the tunnel between Sloane Square and Victoria. The tarmac sea of the park off the Highway near our house, and the peeling paint on the rotting barges moored on the

Thames outside our bedroom window. I loved the sheer messiness of London, the crumbling wharves around Wapping Wall, where a friend held parties in a huge studio, and the empty, disused wharves of Rotherhithe.

I plunged straight back into work – in spite of announcing earlier in the year I wouldn't write about fashion any more, I oversaw a couple of fashion shoots for the *Observer* magazine because it was a chance to work with Barney Bosshart, an American photographer who specialised in dynamic multi-layered images. Princess Anne's engagement had been announced, and I was commissioned to write a feature for *Over 21*, giving her some marital advice. The hypocritical fact that I treated my own marriage vows as something to be shelved when necessary didn't really bother me. I brazenly wrote, 'How come marriage still exists in liberated, full-frontal, non-prude 1973?' All the women I talked to for the feature were quite frank about the shortcomings of marriage, but they also expressed a fear of growing old alone, of divorce's adverse effects on their children. Although I noted that 40 per cent of all married women worked, many still told me they felt they needed the security of marriage. It wasn't something Princess Anne was ever going to have to worry about, I decided. Secretly, I was absolutely determined that no one would ever be supporting me, married or not.

Tim and I had set up a business partnership, with joint bank accounts, but most of our money was being channelled into renovating the house in Narrow Street. He was getting more and more photographic work, which had started to take him to Europe, especially Paris and Milan. I was building a reputation as an opinionated writer, who occasionally appeared on the radio. I was determined to further my career by broadening the range of people I worked for.

I followed up the piece about Princess Anne and marriage with another for *Over 21* about the fact that cars were designed by and for men, in spite of the fact there were four and a half million female drivers. What on earth was that ridiculous thing in a car called a 'glove compartment'? I railed. What women needed was holders for tissue boxes, rubbish bags instead of ashtrays, decent interior fabrics instead of beige plastic – all ideas which eventually materialised about 20 years later! Lee Bender, owner of the successful Bus Stop boutique was photographed in her Alfa Romeo, Barbara Hulanicki talked about her love affair with the Mini and Mary Quant asked why cars couldn't be remodelled every season, like clothes – she wanted a coffee-coloured Rolls.

I'd only been back a couple of weeks when I received an exploratory phone call and subsequently met two former journalists from *The Times*, assistant features editor Geoffrey Wansell and Deputy Editor Michael Cudlipp, a senior deputy editor. They were involved in setting up Britain's first speech-based commercial radio station, London Broadcasting Company (LBC). It would launch in the Greater London area in October and be based in a new building in historic Gough Square, where Dr Johnson once lived, in the maze of alleyways off Fleet Street. I was asked if I'd be interested in presenting a live show each weekday from 9 a.m. until midday, with a journalist from the *Daily Mail* called Paul Callan. Without thinking about it for long, I happily accepted their offer of a six-month contract at a salary of £4,500 a year, starting at the beginning of September. Michael was to be the chief editor of the station, in charge of output, and Geoffrey my immediate boss, features editor.

My first meeting with Paul Callan didn't go well. He wore a pin-striped suit which rather emphasised his portly frame. He took himself very seriously, which was odd, because his previous experience had been as a gossip columnist, writing about debutantes, Princess Margaret and show-business. Nevertheless, he soon made me feel as if he was the heavyweight journalist in our fledgling partnership and I was the cockney 'fluff', there to add light relief.

In 1973 it still felt as if the old guard were in charge of things. In spite of the student riots and sit-ins of the late 1960s, there were still debutante balls and lords running the country, although two members of Edward's Heath's

government, Earl Jellicoe and Lord Lambton, had resigned from their posts in May when it was discovered that they had paid prostitutes for sex. The *News of the World* had published pictures of Lord Lambton with a call girl, Norma Levy, and he had admitted to affairs with two other women, saying he 'liked variety'. He was found guilty of possessing cannabis and amphetamines and fined £300; his wife declared their marriage over and he subsequently left the country. All this at a time when Lord Longford was campaigning against pornography! We lived in hypocritical times, it seemed to me.

The IRA had begun a new terror campaign when they started sending letter bombs in August, and many businesses in the media had bought scanning machines to ensure the safety of their staff. LBC didn't have the cash – this was going to be the new face of broadcasting, I was told, but unlike the BBC it would operate on a shoestring. Michael and Geoffrey said that Paul and I would be the 'new voices of London', and the idea was to challenge the smug domination of the BBC head-on by doing things in a much more informal way.

Many of the hundred or so journalists and producers recruited to work at the station came from a journalistic rather than broadcasting background, which meant they might be enthusiastic and fresh but they were also pretty useless when things soon started to go wrong. I was no exception, as it turned out. Nevertheless, LBC was launched with loads of publicity as 'London's first all-talk station'. I don't think any of us realised just how difficult it would be to fill 24 hours a day with speech, on a limited budget.

Being me, I had also signed up to another venture, this time with Haymarket Publishing, which was owned by the wealthy Conservative MP Michael Heseltine. The group specialised in business magazines aimed at an upmarket professional readership, and in this respect they were very savvy. They had published the beautiful but ultimately unprofitable monthly glossy magazine for men, *Town*, which had featured Marc Bolan as a mod in all his finery in a great set of black-and-white pictures by Don McCullin, who went on to become a distinguished war photographer.

Haymarket made their profits from niche publications packed with advertising: they produced *Campaign*, the bible of the advertising industry, and other magazines aimed at the public relations and marketing sectors.

Lindsay Masters was Heseltine's publisher, and over a drink he outlined to me their plans to exploit the huge amount of job advertising aimed at young women, by launching a give-away weekly magazine. They had an experienced executive editor, Jim Ferrier, who had worked for the company for some time, but they had no knowledge of how to attract the kind of women readers interested in ads for secretaries. Would I like to come on board? The art director would be Roland Schenk, who had won many awards for his work on *Campaign*.

Although I had already accepted the LBC job, I persuaded Lindsay to let me work for him from two till six every afternoon. I would come off air in Fleet Street at noon, plan the next day's show with the producer, grab a quick lunch, and then get stuck into my new role at the Haymarket offices in Oxford Circus. I had no idea of the workload I was about to take on. We began putting together a series of dummy issues to show advertisers, and it was decided that the magazine would be called *West One*, have a glossy cover and use good paper for the fashion and beauty sections. We'd have to create about 20 pages of editorial a week, which meant a fashion story, readers' letters, a couple of features, a beauty page and

news. For the first time ever, a woman's magazine would not be sold but would be given away at tube stations in central London one morning a week.

I found Jim Ferrier a delight to work with, a charming Scotsman with a great sense of humour. My relationship with Roland Schenk was another matter. There was no doubt he was a designer of the first rank, but from my perspective he had no experience of or natural flair for connecting with our target readership. His approach was too cerebral and formal, too rooted in the cool and intellectual. I decided to try to get Lindsay to appoint as art director Margot Parker, whom I'd worked with on

Petticoat; she had great connections with young photographers and artists, and a very irreverent approach. Luckily, Lindsay agreed. I also found a completely dotty but madly enthusiastic young fashion editor called Prue Walters, who had been a dress designer. Now I felt more comfortable with the project.

Back at LBC Paul and I were starting to put together running orders and trying to book guests for our show, which was to start on the station's first day on air, Monday, 8 October. It was to be called, rather unimaginatively, *Two in the Morning*. There had never been a station like LBC before, so it was hard to explain what it would sound like. Publicists soon realised that it was a great way to plug books, shows, films and plays, and we were offered actors, authors, playwrights and sportsmen. Museum directors and curators leaped at the chance to plug their exhibitions. The trouble was, most of them were about as radio-savvy as I was. Paul and I were given a young producer called Sarah, who had the unenviable task of working with the pair of us. She was very pleasant, but totally inexperienced in live radio. Mind you, the other presenters – Carol Barnes (recruited from *Time Out*) David Jessel, Claire Rayner, the MP George Gale (who was to present a new kind of programme called a 'phone-in' for two hours directly after *Two in the Morning*) and Jeremy Beadle – were all about as experienced as Paul and I were, and that wasn't saying much.

The Independent Broadcasting Authority was making all sorts of ludicrous demands about the technical standards required for the station, demanding that everything be up to BBC level, even though we were a new organisation, with a completely different agenda, aimed at only one bit of Britain, the capital, and did not have to transmit live music or broadcast symphony orchestras. Consequently, the studios were still being built during the vital run-up to our on-air launch, and we didn't have enough run-throughs to iron out technical problems. Paul and I didn't realise, either, that two-handed presenting required a lot of ingenuity and give and take. Thankfully, we were not required to do anything too technical; it was all I could cope with to keep to time and go in and out of the news on the hour and every fifteen minutes.

Unfortunately, the station was being launched during a recession, with the threat of a three-day week looming as Ted Heath failed to deal with the growing energy crisis caused by an oil embargo imposed by the Arab states in the Middle East. The IRA had let off bombs in central London on 10 September, and two days before we launched the Arabs and Israelis went to war. The miners were threatening to go on strike, and the launch of London's commercial music station, Capital, only eight days after we went on air, confused listeners and made it even more difficult for us to attract advertising.

The staff, fed up with working long hours in appalling conditions, threatened to go on strike. One memo written to the management by the union rep said, 'We are often described as the battery hens of broadcasting – we would like parity with battery hens, who do get food, light, heat and water.' The workers wanted to earn the same as their counterparts at the BBC, perhaps failing to understand how strapped for cash the company was.

In September I went to the opening of the new Biba department store in the former Derry and Toms building on Kensington High Street, and Barbara Hulanicki and her husband, Fitz, held a party in the art deco Rainbow Room. I'd never seen such lavish 1930s marble toilets anywhere – they alone were worth the trip to west

London. We went to see the Rolling Stones play at Wembley Stadium – Mick Jagger wore a jumpsuit designed by Ossie Clark, who had ended his partnership with our old friend Alice Pollock. The atmosphere at Wembley was electric. We also went to Richard O'Brien's new musical, *The Rocky Horror Show*, which transferred to a former cinema in the Kings Road from the small studio theatre upstairs at the Royal Court. Our friend Nell Campbell, a lively Australian tap dancer, had her big break in it. The opening ended with us getting completely drunk at a party in a big studio off Kensington Church Street. I thought I would have to cut back on this kind of life during the week with my new work schedule – but of course I didn't.

Luckily, the first *West One* came out on 23 October, so I had a couple of weeks to get into my new routine at LBC. I got up at 6.30, washed – I didn't dare have a bath in case I fell asleep in it – and then lay on the bathroom floor, fully clothed, waiting for the 7.30 cab to take me to LBC, about 15 minutes away at that hour of the morning, although negotiating our way through Billingsgate fish market could cause problems. I'd read a couple of papers en route, looking for ideas, then plough

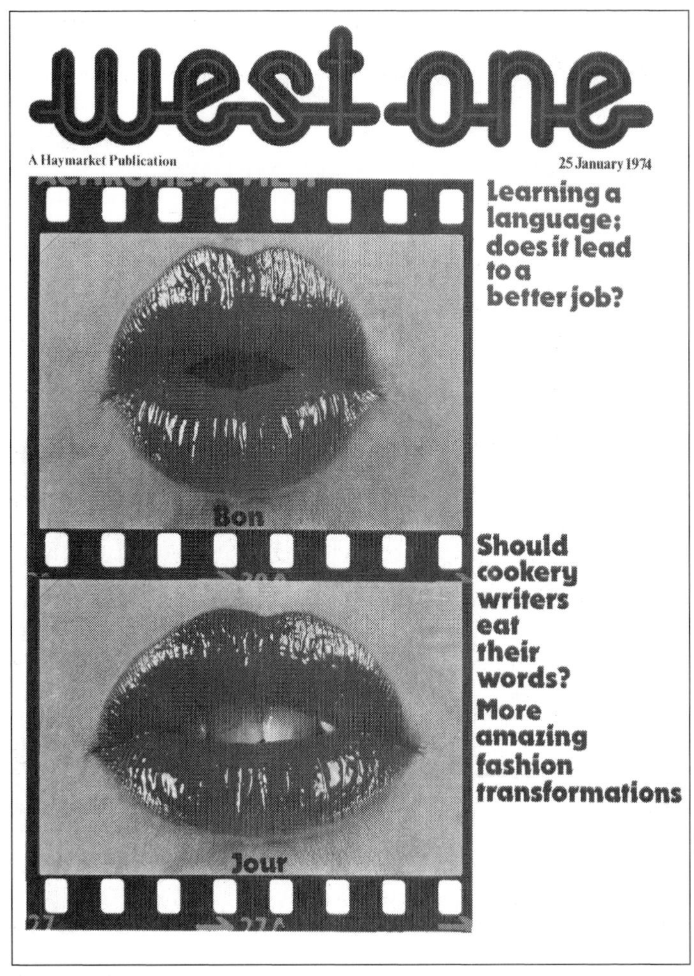

through the rest while eating a doughnut and drinking gallons of black coffee at my desk. With three hours to fill, there would be about three or four guests pre-booked, but once we were on air we had to rely on reading out letters, taking phone calls, talking to reporters out on the road and hoping for some last-minute newsy pundits to liven things up.

Right from the start Paul started to wind me up – and if I'm honest, I did have a very short fuse and a bit of a lack of a sense of humour when it came to jokes about myself. In truth, I was extremely thin-skinned and spent ages at home inspecting myself in the mirror and finding myself wanting. I had very low self-esteem in spite of my exterior bravado. After I messed up reading out the weather (by saying Britain was moving west under a bank of low pressure), that onerous task was removed from me for good. Ditto the traffic news. I could just about manage the news headlines. The desk was full of endless bits of paper, letters from listeners, running orders, books we were meant to have read (no chance of that) and explanations of who our guests were. (We didn't need many because we sat in that studio and abused each other endlessly every day. People would come in and try to get a word in edgeways with great difficulty.) When guests didn't turn up, or were delayed in traffic, Paul would get wound up during the commercial breaks and Sarah would often end up crying in the toilets while we

waffled to fill in the time. It was a bloody nightmare.

Paul used to tell listeners what I was wearing and mock my colourful ensembles – often a bit of a weird combination thrown on while half-awake. He'd reveal I had huge bags under my eyes and was suffering a serious hangover. He implied I hung out with weirdos, while he was part of the establishment. In turn, I moaned about his suede shoes, the stench of the French cigarettes he smoked, his endless harping on about his houses in the country and in 'town'.

Day in and day out, the morning was spent settling scores and trashing each other's taste in everything from food to décor to music to fashion. The listeners were riveted. Soon I had mountains of mail, which divided into my loyal fans, committed to defending me to all and sundry, and the disgusted, who were turning off in droves, appalled by my estuary accent and cheeky manner. The disgusted were enraged that I did not give the plummy-sounding Mr Callan the respect he (to them, at least) deserved.

Paul appealed to the blue-rinse brigade, the middle-aged and middle-class women – in short, the *Daily Mail*'s readers. I was the darling of taxi drivers, ordinary workers, the young and the poorer pensioners. Soon, cartoons about my voice appeared everywhere. *Private Eye* began to mock me. Snotty critics like Julian Barnes and Richard Ingrams started slagging me off in the weekly magazines. And, boy, did the newspaper radio critics despise me! It seemed that every Londoner had to have an opinion – you either liked or loathed Janet Street-Porter and her voice; there was no middle ground. The minute I opened my mouth in a restaurant, in the pub, or in the supermarket, everyone knew who I was – it was a new and thoroughly disconcerting experience.

Paul told people in the newspaper business he thought I was ruthlessly ambitious and I had a terrible temper – both correct. I thought he was a snooty slimeball, something out of P. G. Wodehouse, who toadied up to people who didn't deserve to be taken seriously. He made much of having been to Eton and claimed he came from a comfortable background, implying that I was a common bird crawling up the pyramid of power from the gutter. He certainly took himself and his perceived place in 'society' very seriously.

Less than a week after LBC's launch, I went to the very first Alternative Miss World competition, organised by the sculptor Andrew Logan and held in his studio one Saturday night in Hackney, then alien territory to anyone trendy. The judges summed up the existence of another order, a world Paul Callan and his ilk knew nothing about: designers Ossie Clark, Zandra Rhodes and Barbara Hulanicki and photographer David Bailey. Men and women, gay and straight, old and young – even members of Andrew's own family – all competed, wearing costumes for the two categories, day wear and evening wear, cheered on by a packed audience crammed into the long, narrow space. Andrew wore an outfit which was half white tie and tails, half gold-lamé ruched evening dress. The trophy was one of his mirrored artworks. It was the kind of event Paul would have found disconcerting, unnerving and without merit as no debs or titled people took part, and yet, sitting in that hot, smoky room, I found it exhilarating and captivating. Andrew was one of the most non-judgemental people I'd ever met.

Meanwhile, the relationship I was establishing with my listeners was getting weirder and weirder.

Hi Janet,
I had to write to you. If ever you're in Camberwell, call in at the Mecca Bingo Hall, you will see your double, she speaks exactly like you, and many people have told her that she looks like you. My camera is broken otherwise I would have taken a photo of her. So don't forget to call in if you are ever down this way. PS Don't disclose my name on the air. PPS Call in for a cup of tea if you're ever round this way. PPPS I've enclosed a stamped addressed envelope for you

to acknowledge my letter because I'm bound to be asleep if it's read out on your programme.

All the writers seemed obsessed with my accent, as if the sound of someone's voice was a subject they'd never thought about before. I inspired advice from the helpfully constructive – 'Why not take clarinet lessons to improve your embouchure?' – to the downright rude. I could only assume they had misinterpreted the implications of my double-barrelled name when they'd seen it in print over the past four years, in the *Daily Mail*, the *Evening Standard*, the *Observer* and *Queen*, and now they were going to wreak their revenge on me for having fooled them in some unstated mysterious way.

'Madam: I have been listening to your voice and would suggest that as a Broadcaster you would make an excellent Traffic Warden. Pardon my frankness . . .' And of course they always printed their full name and address, expecting a grateful reply. But it got worse.

Dear Miss Street-Porter,

I am sure you are pleased to know that I commiserate with you completely concerning the continual complaints about your voice and its suggested 'non-appeal' on the wireless. Why people should be wasting their time and money dialling and writing to LBC merely to make some petty complaint about a set of vocal chords and how they vibrate and whether the tongue is projected and contracted correctly is completely beyond my comprehension. What they should be ringing LBC about (and writing with fervour) is the complete lack of any 'grey matter' or intelligence to activate your particular mindless vociferations.

Yours etc

Again, sent with full name and address.

Then there was the short and sweet: 'Please GO OFF OUR AIR. Your voice is excrutiatingly awful. Take a job at LBC as a tea lady or something. How they employed you is beyond comprehension. Yours sincerely.' Even the compliments were back-handed: 'Dear Janet, I enclose a cutting from the *News of the World* for you to read. It says you are refreshing but I do not agree. As a former nurse I feel sure that what you need is an adenoid operation.'

I was also beginning to attract the kind of sexual innuendo I hadn't received since my days at the *Daily Mail*, when I'd kept up a correspondence with a rubber fetishist in Wiltshire, who sent me rubber knickers and a poncho after I had innocently written a fashion feature on rainwear. I had great fun composing the replies, but after a while I would simply stuff the latex garment he'd sent me in a brown envelope and type one word on a *Daily Mail* compliments slip before I signed it and popped it in the post: 'Worn'. I knew that would suffice! Now the nutters were resurfacing as LBC listeners: 'Dear Janette Porter, you are a beautiful girl. Maybe if we get to meet I would be able to possess you or even marry you but I do not want our children to think it is British to speak the way you do.' On the *Mail* I'd received letters from a long-distance lorry driver who found my mug shot (at the top of my weekly column) so appealing that he wrote to tell me he bought the paper every Saturday, licked it until my photo was on his tongue and then swallowed it. Now that sort of thing was happening again: 'Dear Janet, Listening to Paul and you on the radio this morning, I noticed he said you were wearing a green dress. That was especially thrilling as I love all greens. We have so much in common

I am hardly able to keep my mind on plain everyday affairs . . .'

In among the crazies ranting about my accent, my clothing, my glasses and my teeth, were the racists. They usually wrote in block capitals, and frequently drew me with a giant black willy aimed at my open mouth, or an axe sticking out of my back. With the IRA letter-bomb campaign under way in London, soon all the LBC presenters were receiving anti-Irish correspondence: 'LBC BRINGS TWO SURPRISES. THE GREATEST OF THESE IS JANET STREET-PORTER. THE SECOND IS THE NUMBER OF IRISH PEOPLE WHO CALL ALL YOUR PHONE-IN SHOWS.'

My days were spent dashing from Fleet Street to Oxford Circus and back again. After *Two in the Morning* ended at noon, I spent about half an hour with our producer and Paul, trying to think of guests for the next day. Then, if Paul and I were speaking, we'd go to El Vino for a glass of wine and a debrief – how much longer could we cope with this chaos? I'd jump in a cab, clutching a sandwich, and start my afternoon at Haymarket.

West One was looking good – there was plenty of advertising and I had a good team. Soon my title was changed on the masthead from consultant to editor, a sign of Lindsay Masters's confidence. Margot Parker came up with some great covers and Prue Walters was a really talented fashion editor. We had two feature writers, Jane Merer, who'd won one of the *Vogue* talent competitions, and Roger Bingham, a former president of the students' union at London University. In the background Jim Ferrier was a steady presence, keeping our Haymarket bosses at arm's length and helping me not to go over budget. Frederic Davies contributed our horoscopes, and our features concentrated on women and work – always a subject dear to my heart. We did plenty of profiles of good role models, from Audrey Slaughter and Jenny Barraclough (then an up-and-coming documentary maker at the BBC) to Barbara Attenborough, who had designed the No 7 makeup range for Boots.

Margot persuaded some very good photographers and graphic artists to work for us, people like Roger Charity, Philip Castle, John Bishops and Harri Peccinotti, who normally worked for *Vogue*, *Nova*, *Harpers & Queen* and other up-market glossies. We felt we were punching over our weight – looking like something you'd pay decent money for, rather than a give-away rag. We photographed stylish women in their own clothes: Vivienne Westwood (who then owned a shop called Let It Rock on the Kings Road), Suzi Quatro, who'd just had a big hit record, and Diane Logan, sister-in-law of Andrew, the sculptor; she'd just opened a hat shop off Baker Street. We ran consumer-orientated features on how to complain, where to eat cheaply and how to change your career.

Although my time at *West One* was limited, I was totally committed to its mantra of self-help and self-improvement. It was something that had obsessed me ever since my early teens. The world of work was my special subject, something I thought about from morning to night.

My day at *West One* ended at around 6.30, and I'd take a taxi back to Gough Square and check through the plans for the next day, before heading out to a party or dinner. The pressures of both our busy careers meant that Tim and I spent less and less time together, and I took advantage of his frequent trips abroad, to photograph modern buildings all over Europe, to enjoy some secret affairs.

Early in 1974 I'd had a brief fling with a charming art dealer, James. We used to meet at his flat in the early evening, for a couple of hours. One afternoon I was working on *West One* when James called and invited me to spend the weekend with him in New York. Tim was in Italy, working – due back on Monday afternoon – so I figured I could get away with it.

When Tim called I said I was going to the country for the weekend, keeping things pretty vague. I caught the Friday afternoon flight to New York and before long James and I were in a bar drinking with the pop artist James Rosenquist. After supper, we decided to go to see the legendary comedian Mort Sahl at the art deco Rainbow Room – only trouble was, it was completely packed. Luckily one of Rosenquist's paintings had just been used on the cover of the New York telephone directory, and when he agreed to sign a couple of copies, the maitre d' soon gave us an excellent table in the front row. Before 20 minutes was up, we were asked to leave. We weren't laughing in the right places, and were far too stroppy, too engrossed in our own free-wheeling conversation, to give Mr Sahl the respectful silence he expected for his monologues. A short taxi ride uptown took us to James's flat, a tiny walk-up studio, one room with a kitchenette and a bathroom, in the middle of gallery land. I slept fitfully and on Saturday morning my hangover was dreadful, but a heavy-duty art weekend lay ahead. We consumed a gallon of black coffee and ate smoked salmon and cream cheese bagels at the café next door, then I dozed in the car during the hour-and-a-half journey to the Hamptons, where we would be spending the night with Roy and Dorothy Lichenstein in their exquisite white clapboard house outside Bridgehampton.

Roy was at the peak of his fame – his comic-strip-inspired paintings were fetching high prices at auction and museums were queueing up to buy his work. Unlike Andy Warhol, Roy was not a party animal – he was extremely shy and unassuming, and generally shunned the social scene – but an invitation to their house in the glamorous Hamptons was regarded as a social prize. They were easy and relaxed about our somewhat dishevelled arrival, but everything got a whole lot more formal about an hour later when Jackie Kennedy's sister Lee Radziwill arrived for lunch, with the highly successful New York dealer Leo Castelli in tow. Lee looked exactly like a miniature version of Jackie, in a little gabardine mini dress and cashmere cardigan – no concessions to the countryside in her wardrobe.

While the others were chatting in the kitchen Roy took

me over to his studio, a separate clapboard building (once a barn), where he was working on a series of canvases based on Léger and Picasso still lifes, full of wit and irony. It wasn't a surprise that he and Allen Jones got on well: they had exactly the same sense of humour; and Roy was delighted that I knew such a good friend of his so well. The time flashed by, but after 30 minutes we rejoined the others.

Dorothy was extremely vivacious and was a hoot socially. She had been to cordon bleu cookery school in Paris and was determined to demonstrate her expertise: lunch was quails cooked with grapes in a giant copper casserole. I was very impressed, but Leo Castelli couldn't have cared less about the food, he simply droned on about business with Roy and James throughout the meal. Lee Radziwill just picked at her food – she didn't get that thin by eating much. As I didn't know any of the English aristocracy, she didn't bother to talk to me, assuming, correctly, that I was from a lower social plane.

After coffee, I went upstairs to rest – my head was throbbing with a full-blown migraine. The house dated from the nineteenth century and was beautifully proportioned, but not at all ostentatious, full of elegant wooden furniture and works of art. The guest room contained a smallish antique four-poster bed, with a beautiful old quilt. It wasn't the sort of room you'd have wild sex in, that was for sure. Highly polished wide oak floorboards, whitewashed walls, small pieces of Roy's work on the walls. I took a double dose of codeine, drank several tumblers of water, put a pillow over my head and tried to sleep.

At seven o'clock we assembled downstairs for cocktails – potent martinis. Then a short trip in the car to the beach took us to dinner at the palatial turn-of-the-century mansion of 'Baby' Jane Holzer, a wealthy heiress friendly with many artists and photographers, and with musicians like the Rolling Stones. It was winter and the wind howled outside, and I could hear large waves crashing on the shore. Jane's outfit was extraordinary – a mass of backcombed hair like a lion's mane, loads of sooty black eye makeup, a short skirt, flat ballet pumps. People sprawled over giant cushions, smoking and drinking and talking. I didn't really feel up to it, to be honest. Supper was eaten round a large dining table, maybe 20 people – it all passed in a haze.

Next day after brunch and a walk along the beach with

James, I took a taxi back to the airport and flew home, arriving in London early on Monday morning. Tim was already at the house, furious. 'Where the hell have you been?' he asked. I waffled about going to see Stephen Naab in New York on an impulse. 'You said you were going to the country!' he shouted. 'I didn't say which one,' I wittily replied – but my answer went down like a lead balloon. I had already told Stephen that, if Tim called, he was to provide me with an alibi by saying that I was staying with him – luckily Stephen was uncontactable most of the time, so I was on pretty safe ground. After this episode Tim realised that something was up – and regarded me with suspicion – but we rarely discussed our feelings, and so our relationship was subtly changing. I liked being married, but only on my (rather unconventional) terms.

Within a few months my physical relationship with James had fizzled out, although we remained extremely good friends and often met for lunch or a drink.

One weekend, there was a knock at the front door in Narrow Street. A large, rounded lady introduced herself as the wonderfully named Jacquomine Chabot-Lodvidge.

It turned out that she'd lived in a one-room flat on the top floor of the house when Fred Grunfeld was resident on the first floor, back in the 1960s. Now she worked in feature films, finding locations, and she thought our house might be right for a project being developed by the Italian director Michelangelo Antonioni. She came in and had a coffee.

There had been quite a few changes to the place since we'd moved in. For a start, all the boats and barge-repair stuff had been removed from the ground floor, which was now Tim's studio and housed a snooker table. The top floor was our bedroom, with an art deco bathroom. The whole of the first floor was about 65 feet long and the focal point of this vast space was the old wooden windows and doors, which faced south, opening onto a fabulous balcony over the river, right at the very outside of the curve between Wapping and the Isle of Dogs. I didn't think there was a better place to sit in the evenings anywhere in London.

The room had the original bare brick walls, painted white, a bare timbered ceiling and bleached pine boards on the floor. The furniture was an eclectic mixture: an imposing sycamore glass-topped art deco dining table and chairs, originally made for the founder of Tesco, Jack Cohen, the curvy cloud-shaped three-piece suite we'd got for nothing in Fulham Broadway and had reupholstered in Biba soft-pink cut velvet, and there were a couple of large squishy sausages that any guests could crash out on. Angular glass display cases from Derry and Toms housed my large collection of 1920s advertising fans and bizarre-shaped teapots by Susie Cooper and Clarice Cliffe. On the walls were pop prints by Joe Tilson and Allen Jones.

I had met Antonioni before, when he came to the

Architectural Association in 1965 and persuaded a gang of us to appear as extras in his movie about swinging London, *Blow-Up*. I wore my own clothes (weird red-and-yellow-striped PVC trousers and a silver leather coat) and dyed my long hair silver. I managed to score a larger fee than the others (something like the princely sum of £38 a day!) because I appeared in a scene in a nightclub dancing with a black guy while the Yardbirds played – apparently I qualified for 'action money'.

Jacquomine asked if we would consider renting our house out for Antonioni's new film, *The Passenger*, starring Jack Nicholson, Maria Schneider and Jenny Runacre. She promised to return in a couple of days.

Antonioni had always had the reputation of not being able to speak very good English, but when I answered the front door to him, he broke into a huge smile and said, 'I've met you before!' We reminisced about *Blow-Up* and the way all the penniless students had stormed the tea and doughnut trolley every morning. Most of *The Passenger* was being shot in North Africa, but our house was to be the 'love-nest' where an antiques dealer lived. Antonioni declared himself very pleased with the location, and we did a deal – I think it was about £1,000 a day for three days, which was more than welcome in our household.

He then set about building a camera platform on a gantry on a disused crane housing in the Thames just to the west of our balcony. The structure was not connected to the shore, so first of all they had to construct a bridge to it. Then scaffolding was erected and a camera mounted about 100 feet above the water – it looked extremely precarious. Then Antonioni changed his mind about the fictional antiques dealer who was to 'live' in our house – it seemed our furniture was too 'amusing' and 'ironic' and Mr Antonioni had decided the chap would live with much more macho stuff. So everything in our living room was carefully packed and stored in a lorry down the street, and in came overstuffed leather Chesterfield sofas, dark wood writing desks, tables and chairs, a huge globe, a dark-patterned Persian carpet, lots of brass and a rich dark brown colour scheme. Next, our bedroom, where a bit of bonking was to take place, had to be re-styled: the white walls were sprayed lime green and horrible net curtains blocked out the wonderful view. When the set decorators had finished, we threw a drinks party for our friends in our 'new' home, the night before filming started.

Over the next few days, we got up really early and vacated the premises, going off to work and leaving the film crew to get on with it. There were in fact two crews, because the English unions had objected to Antonioni's Italian technicians, and so a British crew sat around most of the time, being paid to do very little. There were two catering vans parked in the street, with different menus – English and Italian – for the two camps. The locals had a field day, queuing up and consuming as much free grub as they could get away with!

When the film was released in 1975, it didn't get the best of reviews. Critics found the labyrinthine plot (Nicholson plays a TV reporter who takes on the identity of his dead friend) incomprehensible. I dozed throughout, waking only to marvel at how a week in Limehouse had been turned into just a few short minutes in the finished film. But the money meant we could proceed with our refurbishment plans, and we bought a bright red circular plastic shower, which we installed on the ground floor – it was a bit like Doctor Who's Tardis – and we sprayed the hall and staircase with black, green and scarlet glitter. Disco time!

Meanwhile, things were getting worse at LBC – there was a constant threat of strikes. Two people had apparently been caught having sex in one of the unfinished studios in the middle of the night. The offices looked like a bomb had hit them because they were used by messy teams of journalists, presenters, news reporters and producers 24 hours a day. The problem was, LBC had no advertising to pay the staff and the running costs, and the real panto was being acted out off-air.

I went to football at Millwall every couple of weeks with one of our reporters, John Lloyd, as he was a friend of an Irish player, Eamonn Dunphy, who had just been bought by the club. Eamonn would get us into the directors' box, which, as this was Millwall and not a glamorous club like Chelsea or Tottenham, meant we were sitting not far from quite a few shady-looking characters. When Millwall played Fulham one Saturday, I took my dad along. The moment Fulham got their first corner, he stood up and shouted, 'Go on, Fulham!' at the top of his voice. I thought we were going to be lynched, and dragged him back down. He kept quiet for the rest of the match, thank God, and we managed to get away without any further trouble.

During the games John and I used to discuss what on earth was going to happen at LBC – we both realised that the current situation couldn't carry on for much longer. There seemed to be industrial turmoil on all fronts. By November the miners, railway workers, electrical and power workers had all banned overtime, and on 13 December emergency measures to conserve fuel were passed in Parliament; a 50mph speed limit was imposed, temperature controls were imposed in offices, and a three-day working week was introduced.

Suddenly there were management upheavals at LBC. Our Canadian investors decided that, as we had no advertising and spiralling costs, it was time for radical changes. The managing director, Michael Levete, departed and the chief editor, Michael Cudlipp, was replaced by Marshall Stewart. Geoffrey Wansell got promoted. Instead of feature programming, the station was to focus on rolling news, in a British version of a format which was already extremely successful in North America. Paul and I were told that to cut costs we would have separate shows, and George Gale's phone-in would start earlier. My initial six-month contract was set to run out at the end of Feburary and it was renewed for a year (at a salary I had previously negotiated with Michael Cudlipp of £5,000). My new slot, an interview-based show with famous people, was to start at the beginning of March and would run from 6.30 to 7.30 each evening. Paul was given a show running from 7 to 10 a.m. on Saturdays and Sundays, focusing on leisure. I was mightily relieved that our partnership was being axed.

The furore about my accent refused to die down. Richard Afton was a former BBC producer who wrote about television in the *London Evening News*. He decided to write a whole column attacking me, even though radio was not his brief – the editor must have realised that LBC was something a lot of readers listened to, and newspapers in general were hostile to commercial radio, fearful that it might take away some of their advertising revenue (it didn't). Afton wrote:

> Mrs Street-Porter has the most appallingly vulgar accent I have heard outside a low comedy show. This lady – an obvious Women's Libber – achieves the

> impossible by speaking in an adenoidal voice punctuated by sucking noises. It sounds as if she were consuming a plate of spaghetti with a fork and spoon. Add to this a cackling noise reminiscent of a frightened goat and you have the picture. I find it offensive and if the poor lady cannot help it, she should not be on the air . . .

I cried in the back of the cab on my way to *West One*. It didn't matter that Paul Callan was described in the same column as 'the lesser of this dismal duo . . . who speaks in a plummy monotone, and appears to end each sentence with the letter M as in mmmm . . .' My postbag increased and my fans took to sending me copies of the hate mail they'd penned to Mr Afton: 'Your attempt to describe her voice as offensive and vulgar betrays your own narrow-minded thinking and class arrogance.' 'Your double fear of strong and intelligent women as well as the working class is painfully apparent.' Now people were talking of launching a campaign to support me, the last thing I needed: 'Dear LBC, can we please sponsor a BE NICE TO JANET WEEK?'

Paul and I presented our last show together on 28

February 1974, a Thursday, and listeners phoned and wrote in by the dozen to complain: 'Dear Janet and Paul, I am devastated by that goodbye – I found you the best thing I ever heard on the radio. I am feeling very deprived by the thought of not being able to have that pleasant few hours every day. Yours in tears, Peggy.' 'Dear Janet, You and Paul have been part of our family, and I hate changes, being a Capricorn.' 'I shall miss your programme very badly – the inspiration of putting you two together was someone's miraculous idea . . . I SHALL MISS YOU.'

Events outside the hothouse atmosphere of LBC were grimmer than ever. The three-day week meant everyone felt cold and miserable, and getting to and from work was a struggle. The miners had failed to reach agreement in their talks with the prime minister, Ted Heath, and went on strike at the beginning of February. The pound slumped to its lowest level ever against the dollar, and inflation reached 24 per cent. A general election was called on 7 February, but the results indicated no outright winner on 28 February. Jeremy Thorpe, the Liberal Party leader, declined to form a coalition with the Tories, so Harold Wilson was summoned to Buckingham Palace and asked to form a government. The miners called off their strike on 6 March and the three-day week ended the same day.

Rolling news was obviously a sensible direction for LBC to take. Besides all these upheavals, there was a huge amount happening, with pub bombings masterminded by the IRA and the kidnapping of the American heiress Patty Hearst by the self-styled Symbionese Liberation Army in California. The Russian author Aleksandr Solzenhenitsyn had fled his country to live in exile in Europe. The Watergate hearings were still under way in America, and Nixon was resisting impeachment and clinging to power.

I switched my days round and now worked at *West One* in the mornings. I managed to get some really good guests on my new LBC show, and we could sometimes pre-record them, which made my hectic schedule a bit easier. I interviewed Ken Russell about his film of the Who's rock opera *Tommy*, and talked to the actor and writer Peter Ustinov. The controversial architect Colonel Seifert, who had designed London's highest office block, Centre Point, gave me his first radio interview. His landmark remained empty and was a focus for demonstrations about the plight of the homeless. The author

Gore Vidal and the actor James Stewart both plugged their latest books, as did former pop star Heinz.

One of the spookiest men I met during the run of the show was the Paraguayan student Nando Parrado. He'd been a passenger on a plane which crashed in the Andes and had had to eat the raw flesh of his dead friends in order to survive. His story had been turned into a brilliant book called *Alive* by Piers Paul Read. After the interview, with his friend and fellow survivor Robert Canessa, Nando asked me if I would like to go out to dinner with him that night. He was very good-looking, but I declined.

It pained me to admit it but I secretly missed being in a studio with Paul. The best thing we'd done together was a recording with some of the Goons at the Eccentric Club off Pall Mall, at a party to launch the publication of a book of the scripts of the shows. After a (thankfully) brief introduction by Prince Charles, the party really got going and Harry Secombe, Michael Bentine and Spike Milligan reduced Paul and me to hysterics. The taped interview made a great piece of radio next morning. In that situation the chemistry between us had been good.

During the time we worked together Paul went out of

his way to emphasize his upper class credentials. But in many respects he was just as working-class as I was. It was mystifying. Why did he go to such lengths to promote his posh persona? Maybe he felt it was the only way to get on in Fleet Street?

As for me, the myth Paul had perpetuated on the airwaves – that I was a cockney – was equally spurious. I am half Welsh. I grew up in a working-class home in Fulham, west London, but I had no more in common with cockneys born within the sound of Bow Bells than Paul had. I spent my childhood reading, working in the library after school, going to the opera and the ballet with my godmother. By the time I was 18 I was well-educated, and I easily won a place at college to study architecture. But Paul and I had both airbrushed our backgrounds out of our lives – we had that much in common. I was no longer friendly with anyone I'd been at school with, and saw very few of my relatives.

Even my marriage to Tim, on the outside a great match with someone I shared many interests with, was beginning to crumble. At LBC I'd interviewed Ted Simon who was about to go around the world on a motorbike and write a book about his travels. He was a former journalist on the *Sunday Times* who'd written a book about the Formula One grand prix. In his biker's leathers and boots he was a complete turn-on. Unfortunately, the minute he left the studio he was leaving the country and it would be a long time before I saw him again, but the fact that I even considered sleeping with him showed how ambivalent I was about my marriage.

Chapter 7

In March 1974 the *Observer* asked Tim and me to go to Japan to cover an historic event – the first time the English had taken on the Japanese at judo, in their own country. Through the photographer Terry Donovan, a black belt himself, we were introduced to the team's captain, and he arranged for us to stay with a mate who'd married a Japanese girl and now lived in the Tokyo suburbs. It was a fantastic experience from start to finish.

Most of the blokes were in their 20s and had never visited the Far East. Some found the food a real problem, others were soon slurping down bowls of noodles just like the natives. Tim and I became adept at finding our way around the Tokyo Underground system – rush hour was never really a problem for us as all the bodies seemed to be crammed around our waist area. Allen Jones was having a big exhibition while we were in town; to my surprise it took place on the fourth floor of one of the biggest department stores in the Ginza shopping district, not in a gallery – apparently this was the norm. The opening was a prestigious affair, attended by plenty of wealthy businessmen, including senior Sony executives and various product and fashion designers.

What was interesting was how few women were present. Allen's work, with its fetishistic images of big-breasted women in high heels, skimpy pants and startled expressions, obviously turned these chaps on, but we discovered that in Japan businessmen never took their wives out in the evening. The dinner afterwards, given by the British Council, was an all-male affair. Tim and I met the designer Issey Miyake, who was a charming man, and arranged to meet the following night. Even then his clothes were totally original and sculptural. He was the most intellectual dress designer I'd ever met, obsessed with creating new kinds of textiles using cutting-edge technology.

Staying in a Japanese household was a novel experience, starting with our morning routine. We got up at seven o'clock and showered before getting into a very small tub of boiling hot water. Then, forget egg and bacon – now we breakfasted on a variety of small dishes containing stewed eel, sliced raw fish, noodles, pickles, soup and boiled rice.

The judo bouts took place in a large training hall, where the traditional art of kendo was practised on another floor and you could hear the thud of the long batons hitting each other. I was not allowed to enter that room and watch – kendo was considered the most traditional and therefore sacrosanct of all the Japanese martial arts, and female spectators were not welcome. Time and time again I was reminded just how male Japanese culture was, and how women were expected to fit into a pre-determined, servile role.

I found the scoring of the judo tournament completely incomprehensible, as did Allen, who sat with me behind the long trestle table of judges. In the end, the British team suffered the predictable defeat, but it was by no means a walk-over. Afterwards we went for a drink to celebrate and then Tim and I caught the subway back to the suburbs and ordered a massive delivery of sushi, brought by a boy on a bike with circular straw panniers specially designed to hold a tempting array of different fish.

For the second week of our visit we'd been invited to stay at the British embassy – I'd met Simone Warner, the ambassador's wife, through a mutual friend in London, the dress designer Serena Shaffer. The residence was palatial to say the least, a fake Queen Anne brick mansion with an imposing entrance flanked by cream columns, set in about four acres of lush green parkland with a small lake. In Tokyo, where every square metre was built upon, the spaciousness of the embassy's setting was astonishing (our room turned out to be the size of a small council flat).

We arrived in a taxi and were warmly greeted by Simone. Fred, her husband, was resting, as he'd strained his back. She begged me to go and cheer him up. I went upstairs, knocked softly on the dark oak door and opened it quietly. Fred was sprawled across a huge bed, propped up on mounds of dark velvet cushions, wearing a Rolling Stones tour T-shirt and engrossed in *Rock Dreams*, a cult paperback by Nick Cohn and the French artist Guy Peellaert, which showed a series of musical icons in the unlikeliest of situations.

'Janet, darling,' said Fred, '*wonderful* to see you.' Fred was at least six foot tall, thin, with a long face and grey hair. He had the boomiest voice you could imagine. I adored him. He was gregarious, a great host, huge fun, curious about everything. I couldn't imagine for one moment what the Japanese made of him! Nevertheless, this was Britain's emissary in Japan, and what a stylish one he was, too.

We immediately planned a trip later in the week to the world sumo wrestling championships in Osaka. All the tickets were sold, but Fred managed to pull strings and get us a box.

When I asked Fred about laundry, he said, 'Just chuck it on the floor, darling – you'll never have anything so beautifully laundered again!' I went back to our room and emptied the entire contents of our battered Globetrotter cases on the floor, before going down for drinks and dinner. Next day even my white Marks & Sparks cotton knickers were folded like precious pieces of origami. Fred was right – this was a one-off experience I would never forget. There were sixteen servants, endlessly polishing, cooking, washing and folding. I was in heaven.

We invited the judo team over for tea, and Fred and Simone did them proud, laying on egg sandwiches, sausages, loads of sponge cake – a completely British blow-out. The lads, who were sick to the back teeth of rice, noodles, raw fish and bits of artistically cut squid, were ecstatic. After the feast, we celebrated with a cut-throat game of croquet. I interviewed Simone, and Tim photographed her teaching the team the finer points of the game on the lawn – the piece later appeared in British *Vogue*.

On our return to England I picked up a copy of *Harpers & Queen* at the airport and read a feature called 'Young Turks' about up-and-coming single (i.e., eligible) businessmen. I was intrigued by the soft-focus picture of a young man called Tony Elliott, with slightly crossed eyes, a wistful expression and long hair.

Reading that article in the cab from Heathrow to Limehouse, I was fascinated by the story of the public-school boy, exactly the same age as me (we were born within a couple of weeks of each other), whose father had been absent during most of his childhood. His mother, a highly intelligent doctor, had brought up three children by herself.

Tony had gone to Keele university to read French, but left after three years to set up his own magazine, *Time Out*, which he put together on his mum's dining table in her flat on Gloucester Road, financed by a loan she had given him of £75 to get him started.

In the photograph Tony looked boyishly seductive and when our paths crossed a few weeks later the attraction

was mutual and intense. The occasion was a party in a large flat in a mansion block in Knightsbridge, after the opening of an exhibition at the Victoria and Albert Museum which had included some of Tim's photographs, the first he had sold to the museum for their permanent collection. So it was time to celebrate, and the room was full of staff from the museum, designers and photographers. I went up to Tony and introduced myself. He was rather self-effacing and shy – I would soon learn that he was socially inept – but that only made him even more attractive. He had no small talk whatsoever. We arranged to meet for lunch at Bianchi's in Soho. Before long I was sneaking off to his flat in Primrose Hill.

In May my contract at LBC came to an end. I wasn't sorry. I'd spent six months doing a show five days a week, and was tired of all the office politics, the general lack of cash, the turmoil. Many of the people I'd started with the previous September had left, and the original feeling of camaraderie had evaporated as the station rebranded itself, focusing on a news-based agenda. The hours of aimless chat and bizarre time-filling guests plugging everything from movies to macramé were over. I never worked with Paul Callan again.

At the end of June Haymarket decided they could not continue with *West One* any longer. The free magazine market had become crowded and there just weren't the ads to fund all these publications. It was a great shame, because I had worked with such a good team – we had been nominated for awards, and Margot Parker, the art director had produced brilliant covers and stylish layouts. I was sorry the project had to end, but realistic, because Haymarket were an extremely profit-driven organisation and wouldn't carry anything that lost money.

Tony, like me, was a complete workaholic, and spent every hour of the day in his office in Kings Cross. I enjoyed hearing all about his staff, a bunch of left-wing mouthy journalists who insisted on all being paid the same – much to his annoyance, making it impossible to sack anyone in the 'collective'. Tony's closest friend was the co-editor of *Time Out*, David May, who was convinced that the police were bugging his phone because of all the left-wing agit-prop stuff they carried in the magazine.

I met the editor of the *Evening News*, Lou Kirby, who offered me a weekly column starting in September, and Tony asked me to help him set up a new monthly magazine based on 'Sell Out', his consumer section. He rented offices in Charlotte Street because he didn't want it to be staffed or run in the same way as *Time Out*. He naively thought that the *Time Out* union would not interfere.

Tim and I had agreed to go on holiday in Tuscany in July, staying at the farmouse owned by the artist Joe Tilson and his wife. By the time we got there – in the hills just outside Cortona – it was sweltering and there were loads of mosquitoes. The whole area seemed to be swarming with media folk, from Germaine Greer to John Pilger, the *Daily Mirror* war correspondent. Although I got on well with the Tilsons, and particularly liked their three children (we wrote to each other regularly for four years), I couldn't cope with Pilger and his giant ego and the interminable political rows over dinner. I enjoyed sightseeing – Siena, with its sage-green marble cathedral was spectacular – but it was far too hot to enjoy the architecture properly. After three weeks, we flew back to England. I managed to come up with an amazingly complicated lie about needing to go directly to the dentist. Tim dropped me off in Hammersmith and I got a taxi from there straight to Tony's flat. I had really missed him.

Now I was working in an office on the top floor above a shop just off Charlotte Street, which consisted of just a couple of rooms and a loo on the landing. It was pretty basic – just trestle tables and cheap stacking chairs – and there Tony and I spent hours trying to work out how to turn the 'Sell Out' section of *Time Out*, which had been brilliantly put together by Lindsay Bareham since it had started, into a full-blown monthly consumer magazine, focusing on everything from shopping to restaurants. The emphasis was to be on value for money – how to get the best with limited cash. My affair with Tony continued, and Tim was increasingly suspicious.

I started writing for the *Evening News* – I had signed an initial contract for twelve weeks at £100 a column, plus the measly sum of £15 a week expenses. If my contributions were considered a success, my contract would be renewed at £120 a week.

Tony asked me if I would go away for the weekend with him, down to David May's cottage in the Forest of Dean. I devised a cock and bull story about needing to go and work on *Sell Out*, claiming that we were having a working session to generate ideas. With hindsight, I can see that Tim didn't buy that rubbish for one minute. But at the time I was surprised when he turned up late on Saturday night at David's cottage and confronted me. He had simply rung the *Time Out* switchboard on the Friday and found out where we were all going – it wasn't exactly high-level detective work!

He told me if I got my stuff and got in the car with him within ten minutes, he'd drive us back to London and it would be OK – he'd never discuss tonight or Tony and me again.

'What do you mean, "ten minutes"?' I asked petulantly.

Tim said nothing, but turned, got back into the Porsche and closed the door, resting his head on the seat back and shutting his eyes.

I went inside the house and closed the front door.

I spent the next 15 minutes ranting and raving about the general unfairness of time limits, how I needed longer to think about the situation. Tony watched in silence from the sofa. David and his girlfriend hid in the kitchen, too scared to come out. The only sound outside the cottage was the hooting of an owl in a tree nearby. It didn't calm me down. In my fury I suddenly heard the roar of the Porsche. Tim was gone.

I'd blown it. My marriage was definitely over this time.

Tony and I returned to London the next day, and I stayed the night at his small basement flat just off Primrose Hill. I rang Narrow Street, but there was no answer. I spent the whole night awake, going over what had happened. What a stupid way to end my marriage.

On Monday morning I went into the Charlotte Street office, walking through Regent's Park, past the outskirts of the zoo, down the Broadwalk, through the Rose Garden, trying to sort out my thoughts. What on earth was going on? It was high summer, 1974. I had been married for nearly seven years to a man I still really adored. The only trouble was, I seemed incapable of being faithful to him. I'd always got away with it before – but now I had been well and truly found out.

When I arrived at Charlotte Street, Tony called from the *Time Out* offices in Kings Cross to tell me that around 40 black plastic rubbish bags of my belongings had been dumped in the reception area, by a van driver organised by Tim, much to the staff's amusement. Needless to say, the story appeared in 'Londoner's Diary' in the *Evening Standard*. Tony had the bags sent up to Primrose Hill and I tried to cram them into his two-room flat as best I could. Now I was stuck with Tony, whether or not he or I really wanted that – our affair had become public in the most embarrassing way.

The truth was, I had been enjoying a secret relationship with a sexy magazine publisher for a couple of months, but who knows how it would have played out in the long term? Tim's actions brought everything to a dramatic conclusion. I was homeless, because Tim refused to speak to me or let me back into the house, which we jointly owned. Also, we were registered as a business partnership, so our finances were inextricably linked together. I

should have found somewhere to live and given myself some breathing space to decide what I really wanted, but stupidly I did not; I decided to impose myself upon Tony. We were so similar, both obsessed with work; we liked the same music, and often went down to Dingwalls Club in Camden Lock after supper. I really got on with Tony's ex-girlfriend, Caroline, and we went up to Scotland to stay in her house on a lonely peninsula on the west coast of Argyll. Our affair blossomed, although Tony was adept at hiding his feelings and terrified of expressing any emotion, probably because of how badly his father had treated his mother. His mother, Katherine, loathed me – well, nothing new there: I'd been through that with the Street-Porters. She thought I wasn't good enough for her son, plus they had a very close relationship, especially as she'd displayed such enthusiasm for *Time Out* in the early days, to the point of guaranteeing his bank overdraft for his rental business.

We spent the next few months cooped up in very small spaces – the flat – and the office, although Tony split his time between the main *Time Out* offices (where they were increasingly suspicious of his expansion plans) and Charlotte Street. Gradually, my friends came to accept him, and we were invited to dinner with the same people as when I'd been with Tim. Tim and I didn't speak at all for a couple of months, and then I started trying to get him to let me buy his share of the house – he refused, and carried on living there, although his work often took him abroad.

At Christmas, Tony and I decided to take a break in the Caribbean, and flew to the island of Nevis, where we stayed at the Montpelier Plantation Inn, high on a hill above the sea, with an overgrown tennis court and basic but comfortable rooms. My mother, who was absolutely furious about the breakdown of my marriage, gave me a particularly heavy package and insisted that I take it all the way to Nevis and open it on Christmas Day. It turned out to be two cut-glass grapefruit bowls! I remembered how hostile she had been to Tim in the first place, when I broke off my engagement to Rex back in 1965 – ten years later our relationship seemed just as fractious. Maybe it was jealousy on her part – because I was clearly having a lot of fun. Who knows?

I was having trouble with the *Evening News*, too – they were fighting a losing circulation battle with the *Evening Standard*, and were constantly rewriting my copy, sometimes so that it bore little resemblance to what I had filed. I got loads of letters from readers – all those months at LBC had really paid off – but I couldn't see why the *Evening News* had signed me up if they wanted to turn my opinions into bland mush. I began an acrimonious correspondence with Louis Kirby, the editor, who had the cheek to tell me that they were renewing my contract, but not increasing the money – though they would pay me another £5 a week towards my expenses. One of their frequent complaints was that I filed my copy late – and when they rang *Time Out* the switchboard was engaged. It was pitiful, really. But because I needed the cash I had no choice.

I was also writing the odd piece for the *Observer* magazine. One of my assignments took me down to Windsor to spend the day with Rod Stewart, whose house was being featured. I got there at 11 a.m., as directed, and he wasn't out of bed. I wasn't even offered a cup of tea or coffee. At noon, he appeared and I got down to work – he was sulky but I could handle that. By four o'clock I was ravenous. Finally, I asked for something to drink, and I got a cup of tea and one biscuit. The day ended with a photo shoot in his snooker room, which was carpeted in tartan. I'd been taught how to play by a professional a few years before, for an article I wrote for the *Evening Standard*. I'd bought a full-sized table, which was installed at Narrow Street. On the ground floor, I had spent hours playing after dinner with Tim and our friends, and consequently, I wasn't at all bad, beating Rod

Stewart quite easily. He was absolutely furious and retorted sulkily, 'You're not supposed to do that in my house.' After three frames I was 2–1 up and, apart from being faint with hunger and desperate for a drink, I realised it was best to leave as quickly as possible.

One of the funniest things about the interview was his reluctance to admit how camp he had looked when he started out. I used to see him play at the Marquee, and his backcombed hair and tight navy-blue leather coats were quite something. But even mentioning those early days brought on a major strop!

The first issue of *Sell Out* appeared in mid-March 1975, at about the same time as my contract with the *Evening News* ended. That first issue wasn't completely successful – the design left a lot to be desired – but *Sell Out* was definitely a good idea. The trouble was, did Tony have the money to allow it to develop gradually? He had no investors, and no advertising budget outside using pages in *Time Out* to promote it. While we waited to see if sales were good enough to warrant going on to a second issue, he asked me if I would help out at *Time Out* as deputy editor – he felt the magazine was too serious, too news-based, and did not have enough features and consumer stuff. Tony had been unhappy with the direction the magazine was taking and had paid off the joint editors, David May and Jerome Burne, taking over the editorial chair himself. The staff were clearly furious that they had not been consulted about this sudden change, and when I went to work in the offices in Kings Cross there was immediate uproar. The staff were also furious that my job had not been advertised, and when Tony refused to do so they threatened strike action, holding continuous union meetings to disrupt production. Vile graffiti about me appeared in the toilets, and they sent me to Coventry, refusing to speak to me. When Tony and other members of the management team produced the next week's issue of the magazine, the staff just continued to hold their endless meetings.

After a couple of weeks the strain was immense. I could see their point of view, but what I couldn't accept was that I wasn't qualified for the job – I'd already put in seven years as a journalist, was a union member, had edited a magazine, written for all the leading glossy magazines, for both London evening newspapers and for the *Daily Mail*. But the fact I was the girlfriend of the owner (Tony) meant that I had received preferential treatment. Nasty stories about me started appearing in the gossip columns of the *Guardian* and the *Evening Standard*, and in the union newspaper, the *Journalist*. Tony was determined to stand his ground, but I had no appetite for a fight with these pygmies and their out-of-date notions of equal pay for all. Tony had wanted me to help out because he was short-staffed, and I was full of energy and enthusiasm, but to the staff I was the boss's tart.

A shareholders and directors meeting was held on 25 April – by now the National Union of Journalists had made the strike official so that it was impossible to get the magazine printed – and it was clear to everyone that I would have to resign. I made an official complaint to the National Union of Journalists about the inaccuracy of the stories in the *Guardian*, and got the backing of many of the people I'd once worked with at LBC – but I thought my position was basically untenable. I couldn't take the public vilification any longer. I didn't have anywhere I could call my own to live, and this mixture of work and sex was absolutely stupid. I went back to Tony's flat after another day of high tension in the office, and was totally distraught, in floods of tears.

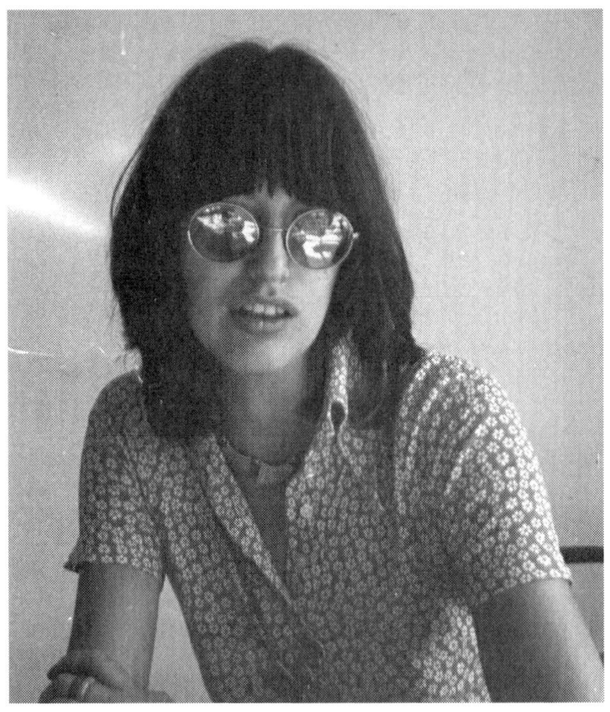

When Tony arrived home and found me he telephoned my mother, and she came over at once with my father. They spent several hours trying to calm me down. I hated to give in to anyone, but this was something else. I also realised that I would never again let bastards like that get to me.

Next day I wrote a letter resigning from *Time Out* and *Sell Out* and took the late-afternoon flight to California, to stay with my friend Joan Quinn in

Los Angeles. I spent two weeks hanging out with her, visiting thrift shops, meeting my artist friends and resuming my friendship with Marc Trabulus, a producer at Paramount.

Tim and I had become very good friends with Robin and Jessie French, who lived in a wonderful old wooden ranch house high up on Coldwater Canyon, on Cherokee Lane. Like Joan, they were art collectors who knew many of the same young artists as we did. Robin was British, had been a very successful agent (it obviously ran in the family, as his father had represented Elizabeth Taylor) and was now head of production at Paramount. Jessie was wonderfully eccentric, a keen fly fisherwoman and talented naive painter. I spent hours on their tennis court trying to improve my serve, coached by an elegant teacher whose silver-grey hair exactly matched his Thunderbird car. I'd met Marc through Robin and Jessie – he was an excellent tennis player, and good company, never lost for words, with a ruthlessly ironic take on life. We used to go drinking in little cocktail lounges where live jazz was played, out in the San Fernando Valley, or go to the Palomino Club to hear country and western artists like Doug Kershaw.

After a couple of weeks at Joan's house – which was a classic Beverly Hills 1920s mansion, built for Oliver Hardy of Laurel and Hardy, it was time to go back to

London. I had started an affair with Marc, but it was nothing serious, just a bit of fun – he lived in a spacious duplex in an old house in West Hollywood. I would stay over at his place from time to time and we'd go for breakfast at Farmer's Market nearby, where all the budding screenwriters hung out.

I arrived back in London to find it was pouring with rain, and Tony was still engrossed in the dispute with his staff. That was enough. I simply unpacked, washed my clothes, repacked and caught the flight the next day back to California. This time I stayed with Marc. The whole *Time Out* strike had had an extremely detrimental effect on Tony's and my relationship – I'd got caught up in his battle to break the stranglehold of the union, which demanded that everyone be paid the same. It was to take him years and another strike before he eventually regained absolute control of his own publication. In May 1981 he fired all the staff and started again three months later with a new set-up. Most of the staff went on to found *City Limits* magazine with financial backing from Ken Livingstone's GLC.

In California, Marc took me to a company called Rent a Wreck – he'd been at school with the owner – and managed to persuade them to rent me their star car, a flamingo-pink Mustang convertible. I'd passed my test after just four lessons on my previous visit, and was not really a confident driver. But I loved the car, and it was just the thing to cheer me up.

In the reception area of Rent a Wreck a miserable-looking man in black was waiting for his car. When he overheard that I was getting the pink Mustang, he started complaining, 'I really wanted that car. It's just so great.' 'Sorry,' I said, 'but we already booked it, and I'm not giving it up – anyway, it matches my hair!' and with that I swept out. Marc was in fits of laughter: I had apparently just given Leonard Cohen the cold shoulder. Well, a pink car wasn't exactly his image, was it?

Marc and I spent a weekend up in Santa Barbara, at the San Isidro ranch, high up in the hills above town – I was really beginning to get to know California now. I went to Nudies Rodeo Tailors on Lankersheim Boulevard out in the Valley – Nudie had made all the great costumes for Elvis Presley, including the famous white jumpsuit he wore in Las Vegas for the live show that was filmed. I bought a leather belt of solid rhinestones with a silver buckle in the shape of a horseshoe – I wore it for ten years until it literally fell to pieces. He also customised a denim shirt for me, embellishing the back with my name in rhinestones – I wore it over and over again on television. Nudies was a fabulous place, totally over the top. He specialised in elaborate embroidery and cowboy boots with silver toe-tips, inset with swirling motifs cut out of snakeskin and alligator.

I was at Robin and Jessie's house one day when I got a phone call from John Birt at London Weekend Television (LWT). Would I come back to London and meet him to discuss presenting a new show for young people? By 1975 I had done plenty of radio, but my television appearances were limited to odd spots on shows like *Late Night Line-Up,* talking about art or fashion. I had seen the groundbreaking television show John had made for Granada television called *Nice Time*, with the unlikely combination of Kenny Everett and Germaine Greer, a funky teatime series with a surreal sense of humour. Now John had left Granada and was working at LWT on the South Bank.

I'd spent about a month in California. It was time to go home and start afresh.

There was no way I was going back to Tony's flat, and

I had been trying to see how I could buy Tim out of the Narrow Street house. By the end of May we had reached an agreement, and so I was about to start on a new chapter in my career, with the security of living in the riverside house I loved. Tony reluctantly agreed to help me pay the mortgage and move in with me. Once again, I was forcing him into something that perhaps he didn't really want to commit to – he had so much on his plate with *Time Out*. By June, we were installed in Limehouse. In September I received a letter of apology from the *Time Out* union chapel, but even that was couched in double-speak: 'Whatever improper behaviour occurred, developed out of a very fraught and rapidly changing situation rather than a planned attack on you.'

I had moved on, and regarded *Time Out* as a matter over and done with. Unfortunately, I lived with the owner of *Time Out*, and so I still heard about all his problems there each and every day. Tim and I resumed our friendship, and he rented a flat in Primrose Hill, bang next door to the house Tony and I had just left.

Chapter 8

On my return to London from California I called John Birt and went up to his office in a tower block overlooking the river on the South Bank.

John was a tall, pudgy bloke with owlish round wire-framed glasses, long silvery-blond hair, a Liverpudlian accent and an intense manner. He was head of current affairs at LWT, but clearly ambitious to build up an empire. His flagship programme was the almost unwatchable *Weekend World*, which was transmitted at Sunday lunchtime and was presented by Peter Jay. Sometimes Peter's questions to the leading politicians of the day were so long and convoluted that viewers must have nodded off. But John was an obsessive, determined to present complicated issues to a wider audience than would normally watch current affairs. He had decided to launch a weekly programme for young people aged 16 to 25, which would run after *Weekend World* on Sundays and would tackle subjects they would be interested in, from music to fashion to sexuality. He introduced me to his friend Andy Mayer, who had worked with him on *Nice Time* and was to be the producer of this new series, and they wanted to know if I would be its presenter.

I realised straight away that John and Andy were right to see that this audience had nothing like this on television for them. Programmes like the incredibly popular *Tiswas* were aimed at younger kids, and were just slapstick fun with no serious content. By using dolly birds with short skirts, cleavage and knee-high boots (like Sally James) to present them, they managed to hook in a fair quota of drooling men as well, but few teenagers. *Smash Hits* and the music press dealt with the charts and new releases really well, but there was nothing looking at things in any depth, going behind the trends to come up with some context and some analysis. It wasn't going to be *Junior Weekend World*; it was going to be a lot more fun.

I took to Andy straight away. A long-haired man in his

late 30s, he seemed at first to be totally self-effacing. He was extremely softly spoken, and prone to mumbling. He also had poor hearing in one ear, to complicate things further. But he was highly intelligent, totally without ego, and open to any ideas at all – he came with absolutely no baggage, which was very energising and exhilarating. In all the years I was to spend working with Andy, he never said, 'You can't do that, because . . .' He only ever said, 'Why not?' London Weekend Television was a place driven by the Light Entertainment empire headed by the bitchy homosexual David Bell. He had Larry Grayson, *On the Buses*, *Mind Your Language* and, the jewel in his crown, Stanley Baxter. The star directors, from Mike Mansfield to Bryan Izzard, were also gay.

LWT came up with some of the highest-rated shows on commercial television in the mid-seventies, and the place oozed confidence. The bar on the second floor was throbbing with life every lunchtime and evening. Even the electricians and scene shifters were on comfortable salaries, reaping the benefits of success. When John arrived in this milieu, with his rather forbidding exterior and high ideals about a 'mission to inform', he must have seemed like a fish out of water. The *Weekend World* team, which included Peter Mandelson with a large moustache and a worrying line in short-sleeved shirts, rarely mixed with the LE mob. It really was a company of two halves.

Our director was another eccentric, a highly talented, tall dark-haired man called Bruce MacDonald, who was prone to epic tantrums if he didn't get his way. At one stage he decided not to wash his hair for a year, and we went through a pretty smelly phase in the cuttings room.

Our programme soon got a reputation as being a place where weirdos hung out. One morning I arrived in the office on the ninth floor of the building and found it completely trashed, typewriters thrown on the floor, pages of script and newspapers everywhere. The door to Andy's office was hanging off its hinges, and stuff had been hurled all over the place. The culprit was never found but we all had our suspicions. Andy managed to smooth everything over with LWT's security men, and the incident was never mentioned again.

The first few episodes of *The London Weekend Show* turned out to be a disaster. Mike Mansfield, who had made his name directing pop shows, was my studio director. I nearly died when he told me I had to walk and talk at the same time! After the pilot episode, they immediately introduced autocue so that my script scrolled up in front of me as I conducted interviews and introduced live bands in the studio, and we played in bits of film I'd shot during the week. Soon, however, Andy got rid of the main use of the studio altogether, only using it for my brief introduction to the film we'd shot in the previous week. In my first year we went on to make well over 40 half-hour programmes, an astonishing amount of output.

I was thoroughly engrossed with the whole process. Andy had assembled a crack team of researchers and assistant producers, from Stephen Scott to Alex Graham to Mike Flood Page, all of whom went on to extremely successful careers in television. They weren't slaves to pluggers and the music press, but had come from journalistic backgrounds and applied the same rigour to writing a script about rent boys and young army deserters as they would to a film about lovers rock or electro pop.

I had signed a contract with John Birt to present the show for £500 a week. After a couple of months I realised that making the show, with two days' filming a week, another day looking at the rough edit of the film and finalising the script, and then more time spent recording the voice-overs and doing the studio introduction, meant that I could do no other work at all.

I decided to confront him about my salary, and booked an appointment for three o'clock one afternoon. When he started getting all pious with me about giving me a break, I lost it and raised my voice, telling him he could shove the fucking job and find some other poor sap to work every hour God sent for that money – I could earn £500 a week writing a newspaper column which took half a day. John got agitated and started telling me to calm down as people on the editorial floor would be able to hear. I promptly stood right next to the flimsy partition wall of his office and screamed, 'Great! I want make sure that everyone on this floor knows what a shit you are!' He asked me to have dinner with him at Chez Victor, a French restaurant in Soho, the following night, and I agreed.

Back in the office Andy was in fits of laughter: 'He's only asked you to dinner in order to chat you up.' I promised to meet Andy and Bruce in the French pub on Dean Street for a full debrief after the dinner.

In the event, nothing happened, although John Birt was considered by many people in the media to be a real ladies' man, in spite of being married to a very gracious and intelligent American, Jane, with whom he had three children. He'd slept with Germaine Greer and had long affairs with two well-known journalists. He certainly didn't excite me. I was concerned solely with getting a pay increase with no strings. I ordered a very expensive bottle of wine – John rarely drank – and over onion soup and steaks we got down to business. I ended up getting £750 a week, to be renegotiated annually. When the coffee came, John was super-keen to sit and chat, but I made an excuse and dashed up the road to meet Andy and Bruce, and soon had them in hysterics.

I was to spend the next two years constantly in minicabs, being ferried from one location to the next all over London and the south-east – we filmed in bus garages, cafés, shops, at speedway tracks and athletics grounds and even in a monastery. Andy was a genius at pulling off a crazy schedule on a limited budget, and we managed to film two, and sometimes three, days a week for one show while editing a second and planning a third. I met Tom Robinson, Vivienne Westwood, Malcolm McLaren and even Arnold Schwarzenegger, who arrived in London to promote a film he'd made about body building called *Stay Hungry*. Andy found a place in deepest south London, Gordon's Gym in Deptford, where young men were busy training in the hope of winning Muscle Men competitions. We persuaded Arnie to pay these amateurs a surprise visit. Even in those days, before he'd made a single blockbuster, Arnie was considered a god in the world of weight training. I kept the lads entertained for an hour while I waited and waited for my surprise to arrive. It transpired that Arnie had suddenly got peckish and the researcher had made the driver stop at a bakery in Camberwell where he had demolished nearly twenty doughnuts! After the filming

Arnie posed for publicity photographs with me sitting on his arm. My hair looks really horrible (in retrospect), a kind of Farrah Fawcett flick round my face with vile yellowy-blond streaks. Arnie doesn't look too different from how he is today, a man with no neck and upper arms the size of bridge supports. Years later, in California, I briefly dated one of his wife's relatives, who was astonished when I turned up for lunch with Arnie to be greeted by the happy cry of 'Hey, babe, how've you been?'

Some of the films we shot were extremely traumatic. We made one full-length documentary about the young rent boys who worked in Piccadilly. The stories they told were extraordinary – and on camera one of them listed all his well-known clients, from a law lord to a famous television presenter. The film had to be destroyed in case it fell into the wrong hands. The boys were mostly on speed or tranquillisers. They hung out by the railings on the corner of Piccadilly and Regent Street – a place known to their punters as the 'meat rack'. We rented a room in a building overlooking the meat rack, put a camera on a tripod and filmed the action day after day.

SPUR

Soon I could read the crowd, the ebb and flow of the bustling throng, and pick out the boys on the game and the middle-aged punters circling them, waiting to strike a deal. We put a hidden microphone on one boy and I heard an American tourist bargaining for a blow job, which would cost him £15 in an alleyway around the corner. Dick Pope, the cameraman on many of the films we shot in 1975 and 1976, built a hidden camera into an ordinary-looking briefcase, and followed the punters and boys in and out of the toilets in the Underground. The boys told me they had wealthy patrons who met them for cocktails in a hotel bar on Park Lane, before sex sessions in car parks and in discreet flats in Mayfair. Many of the boys had run away from home and thought that they could raise their rent money from sex. The trouble was, most of them needed drugs, and some were extremely vulnerable. Few ever escaped from the ritual of selling sex to pay for drugs. The film got on to the front pages of the tabloids   it was a subject that most politicians and the police wanted to ignore.

Another groundbreaking film was about teenage lesbians, a taboo subject on television at any time of day. We filmed a really charming young girl who worked as a bus conductress in the garage off Westbourne Park Road, in the part of London where I'd spent so many Saturdays speaking French and going to Whiteleys department store to buy 'foreign' food with my godmother, Eileen, all those years ago.

Another was about young men who had joined the army and had run away because they couldn't cope – it was a real achievement to get them to talk candidly on camera, when technically they were deserters and could be court-martialled. I spent a couple of days filming young girls who were prostitutes working in Mayfair. We were getting a reputation for tackling difficult and sensitive subjects in an even-handed and unpatronising way, and Andy was always the driving force, keeping a team of stroppy researchers fired up when we were working to a really tight schedule. We made a film about young men who decided to be monks, and we made many documentaries about fashion and music, from rockabilly to the disco scene, reggae and lovers rock.

In November 1975, a few months after the start of *The London Weekend Show*, Tim and I were divorced. He'd had enough of England and was working in Australia, and we resumed a regular correspondence.

Chapter 9

A warm summer's afternoon in late July 1976. We lay in a circle on the rather dusty floor of the large bright room four floors up a tall studio building in East Acton. I closed my eyes and tried (and failed) to meditate. Our group leader was issuing a series of instructions in a low voice, and I dimly heard the words 'focus', 'centred' and 'relax', but I was busy mentally planning what I'd pack to take on a forthcoming trip to America, and where I would be able to go and see the Sex Pistols play in the next couple of weeks. Eventually we were told to breathe deeply, get up, stretch our arms above our heads and sit in a line of chairs, before we started a read-through of a script I had still failed to memorise. This was a rehearsal (an entirely new concept for me, who had spent the last year shooting a 30-minute documentary a week, with little time to read notes, no pre-prepared questions, let alone a chance to actually practise anything in advance).

My new (temporary) boss was the distinguished drama director Philip Saville. He had a well-modulated voice, a distinguished manner, a large nose and crinkly long grey hair. Saville looked more like a professor or an eminent surgeon than an avant-garde television director with a formidable reputation. He'd worked with Harold Pinter for commercial television's *Armchair Theatre* (the play, entitled *A Night Out*, had been watched by 20 million viewers) and he had filmed *Hamlet* on location (a first for the Beeb) in Denmark for the BBC in 1974, and then went on to direct the award-winning series *Boys from the Blackstuff*. The year before we met, 1975, Philip had attracted a lot of attention when he directed a television play called *Gangsters*, shot mainly on location in Birmingham; the result was highly innovative, using footage from violent Asian films intercut with the dramatic action, and it told the story of rival gangs from different ethnic groups within the city. It was the start of a new kind of television – not realistic, but copying different genres like Westerns and mob movies, using freeze-frame techniques and garish colours. Philip Saville was regarded as being in the forefront of technical innovation, someone I'd not only heard of, but whose whole approach fascinated me.

Most TV drama in the 1970s was studio-based, too formal for my taste. I'd been brought up going to see art-house movies with my godmother, and had seen masses of French new-wave cinema. My favourite films were Jean Cocteau's surrealist masterpiece *La Belle et La Bête* (*Beauty and the Beast*), Jean-Luc Godard's black-and-white sci-fi thriller *Alphaville* and a short film, made entirely of stills, about a post-nuclear world, called *La Jetée*, by the French director Chris Marker. I'd also seen most of the Andy Warhol movies at late-night showings at the Electric cinema in Portobello Road, as well as weird stuff made by William Burroughs and Kenneth Anger. I was interested in a different way of telling a story, and Philip Saville was someone I was keen to work with, even if I had zero confidence in my capabilities as an actress. I wanted to be involved in pushing aside the old ideas in television, and thought that maybe I'd learn something from him – a man never frightened of taking risks.

We'd met in April. I'd been filming the *Weekend Show* when I got a phone call from someone called David Halliwell, who said he'd written a play for the BBC and was I interested in being in it? After all the abuse I'd received at LBC about my voice – it still continued from columnists like the horrible old fart Richard Afton in the *Evening News* – I wasn't initially that keen. It was one thing presenting a television programme for young people, filming bands and making documentaries about religious sects like the Moonies and the Children of God, but quite another to have to read out someone else's script and actually play a character. I had absolutely no confidence that I could do it.

I met Halliwell and Philip Saville, who was the director on the project, for a coffee in Patisserie Valerie in Soho. They explained that the drama was part of a series of single plays by different authors, entitled *The Mind Beyond*, the pet project of a respected producer called Irene Shubik. Shubik was known as an innovator who'd made her name at the BBC with work that dealt with science fiction or the supernatural and had said in interviews that she believed in extra-sensory perception. I was fascinated by David Halliwell's script, which dissected the story of a girl called Meriel, who appeared at a séance in Cricklewood. Did Meriel ever exist? Through the eyes of three different sleuths – an underground journalist, a private detective and an investigator of psychic phenomena – the viewer would be taken on a journey of discovery into the world of the paranormal. Philip explained that the play would be shot in three different styles to represent the three main characters.

I was astonished to be told that George Livingstone, the psychic investigator, was to be played by one of my favourite actors, Donald Pleasence, who had been a sensation in Roman Polanski's thriller *Cul de Sac* (released in 1966), filmed on Holy Island off the coast of Northumberland, a bit of bleak coastline I'd visited many times. In the film Pleasence dressed up in his wife's (played by the beautiful French actress Françoise Dorléac) nightie and had his face smeared with her lipstick and eye makeup – I couldn't wait to meet him! His scenes were to be shot in rich, saturated colour, formal in style.

A well-known character actor called John Bluthal had been cast as Sam Nicholls, the private detective. His part of the story was to be filmed in black-and-white, like a parody of a 1930s gangster film. Philip had seen some episodes of *The London Weekend Show* and thought I would be right for the part of Robina Oliver, a journalist on an underground newspaper. My agent, Irene Josephy, was delighted, and set about getting me equal billing and pay with the other two stars, undeterred by the fact that I'd never acted before.

I warmed to David Halliwell. He was a bluff northerner of few words and no social graces. I'd really enjoyed the film of his play *Little Malcolm and his Struggle Against the Eunuchs*, which had opened in 1974 and starred John Hurt in the title role, with David Warner as his sidekick.

Little Malcolm had originally been staged at the Unity Theatre in London in 1965, and received very good reviews, winning Halliwell the *Evening Standard* award for most promising playwright in 1967. It told the story of how Malcolm Scrawsdyke, chucked out of art school in Huddersfield for being a subversive influence, plots his revenge by forming the Party of Dynamic Erection with three of his loyal mates, one of whom (played by David Warner) carried the unfortunate name of Nipple. Malcolm's freezing, bare studio became their headquarters in what they saw as a class struggle against authority, their single aim being the complete humiliation of the teacher who originally expelled Malcolm.

Halliwell's *Little Malcolm* plot seemed to be a mixture of William Golding's book *Lord of the Flies* (turned into a successful film directed by Lindsay Anderson in 1963), which told the story of a bunch of shipwrecked schoolboys who established their own rules in order to survive, and Kafka's *The Trial*. It also captured completely the student protest movement which had led to sit-ins and demonstrations at campuses all over Britain in the late 60s, as students fought for more say in how these temples of learning were run. In *Little Malcolm* Halliwell turned a black comedy into a bleak drama as things started to go terribly wrong for Malcolm and his grandiose plans. I identified with Malcolm in so many ways, having been the permanent protester at grammar school, the girl who loathed rules, railed against the system, hated the restrictions of the established way of doing things. I'd joined the Young Socialists, CND, the Yellow Star movement (forerunner of the anti-apartheid movement) and gone on anti-war demonstrations at the time of the Vietnam war.

There was no doubt, after meeting Halliwell, that he was an extremely left-wing writer, and I couldn't see why he had got involved with the BBC producer Irene Shubik's theories about the supernatural. He was more concerned with social realism than fanciful conceits about the afterlife. But, like Philip, he was someone I was curious to know more about. The only problem I could foresee was that I wasn't a member of Equity, the actor's union, but Irene and Philip filled out all the necessary forms, citing the fact that I'd appeared on television every week for a year. At this time Equity were making a lot of fuss about non-actors taking work from their members, and I just hoped that my application wouldn't get picked up by the press.

In the meantime, I had presented an episode of *The London Weekend Show* which attracted a great deal of attention for a show only broadcast in the London area at Sunday lunchtime. It was because our producer, Andy, had decided that the time was right to look into the kind of religious cults that were attracting our target audience of young people. After the Beatles' flirtation with the Maharishi, there were a whole series of quasi-spiritual groups flourishing in Britain, feeding off young people's search for alternative forms of belief and their quest for a less materialistic, simpler way of life, the fallout from hippies and the counter-culture movement.

There were the Children of God, whose leader, Moses David, never gave interviews, encouraged free love among his followers and published a series of wacky comics. There were the Scientologists, led by a reclusive American, L. Ron Hubbard, with their mumbo-jumbo about dianetics; and the followers of the Indian guru Bhagwan, who believed that through meditation you could actually fly! They had bought a huge Victorian stately home, Mentmore, just outside London for their HQ. Then there was the small band of devotees of Meher Baba whom I'd met through Mike McInnery a few years earlier.

Top of our list were the followers of the Korean mystic the Reverend Sun Myung Moon, whose disciples were known as Moonies. We'd run across some of them recruiting in the West End of London, and their lavish headquarters in Lancaster Gate had cost hundreds of thousands of pounds, even though there were only a few hundred devotees in the UK. The Unification Church, as it was known, encouraged believers to give all their possessions to the organisation, and we had heard from many parents whose sons and daughters had vanished and were thought to be living in communes.

Moon claimed to have been imprisoned by the communists during the Korean war of the 1950s, and had left South Korea to live in a huge mansion in New York State. In America he had attracted thousands of followers and much controversy, but in England he had a much lower profile. We were thrilled to be the first television crew offered the chance to film at the Moonies' estate at Stanton Fitzwarren in Wiltshire, and granted an interview with their leader in the UK, Dennis Orme, at the Lancaster Gate HQ. We rented rooms in the Waldorf Hotel in London, and I filmed a series of very distressing interviews with parents whose teenage children had disappeared into the cult, and who now had no contact at all with them, in spite of numerous letters and phone calls.

I talked to ex-followers, among them one young man who had accepted an offer from a 'cultural foundation' to visit America for just £10. The 'foundation' turned out to be run by the Unification Church, and on arrival at their US headquarters he found that students had to get up at

6 a.m. and had to go through a series of martial-arts-style exercises. They were bombarded with lectures all day and until late at night. He was constantly told about 'the divine principle' during the 40 days, during which all the lectures were repeated three times. The students were not allowed to leave. By the end of his stay many people were disorientated and confused. He had to bow to a picture of Moon daily, and was encouraged to break all ties with his family if he joined the group, treating Moon as his new 'father'. Videos of the Leader's speeches showed that he managed to rant for hours on end to a captive audience of docile disciples.

In Britain, some parents had formed a group called FAIR (Family Action Information and Rescue) in order to try to get their children to leave the Unification Church, and it regularly held meetings at the House of Commons. Attempts to snatch back their offspring had been repulsed by groups of disciples chanting, 'Subjugate, subjugate Satan.'

I met the crew at 6 a.m. in west London and we drove down to Stanton Fitzwarren, a large farmhouse and outbuildings in hundreds of acres of farmland. It had been given to the sect by a convert, Henry Masters, and had previously been in his family for 400 years. We were treated with the utmost graciousness and offered coffee and biscuits. The young disciples seemed very placid, and walked around with enormous smiles plastered all over their faces. They looked a bit washed-out and pale – but I put that down to the vegetarian diet and lack of sleep. The farmhouse was spartan, with bare floors, the kitchen filled by a large wooden table where we drank our coffee. A spacious living room was empty of furniture; just cushions on a rug on the floor and a blackboard. Upstairs, the bedrooms had been turned into dormitories. The Moonies sang a few songs, accompanied by a long-haired person on a guitar. They resumed their classes, which we were allowed to film for a few minutes.

By 12.30 the atmosphere was giving me a splitting headache. They asked if we would like to join them for prayers and soup, but we politely declined, claiming that I had to record some pieces to camera in the fields. The moment we got to the end of the driveway, I burst into hysterical laughter.

The people we were filming were absolutely exhausted, incapable of conversation even if they had been allowed to chat – and it was clear they were not. They had been up since five, and would be spending the day and evening until very late in a monotonous routine of prayer, lectures and very little food. It was obvious that these were sad, lonely kids, glad to be in a club, even if it was one that a lot of people disapproved of. After a couple of drinks and a ham sandwich in the local pub, we returned to the farmhouse to film more chanting, praying and meditation. A man in the pub told me that disciples had been seen ploughing the fields by moonlight!

Back in London Dennis Orme, the Reverend Moon's emissary in the UK, proved to be an unsettling interviewee. He told me that if I manipulated the film and edited it to show him or the sect in a bad light, 'the heavenly hounds would haunt me in my dreams'. Before the camera rolled he put his head in his hands – he was a middle-aged chap in a business suit, inconsequential really. Then, as the interview went on, he started staring at me very forcefully and appeared to be weeping. It was unnerving. He said he wanted to raise £55 million to 'resurrect Britain and teach people to love', on the basis that it would cost about a pound a person to give the

British a spiritual education. We discovered that Mr Orme had formerly been in the merchant navy and had attended Hull University, but we never discovered how a working-class bloke from the north had become linked to a South Korean guru. Mr Orme passionately denied that any members of the sect were brainwashed.

After the programme aired, there were prominent features about it on the news pages of the *Observer* and the *Daily Telegraph* and we received a very complimentary letter from the Independent Broadcasting Authority, saying, 'We feel that the programme and Janet Street-Porter will have successfully communicated the possible dangers of this sect in a style and manner far better than a *World in Action* type of report. We feel that the programme has grown in stature considerably in recent months.'

High praise, but the series in general was still not getting reviewed by most of the critics, even though the subjects we were tackling – notably army deserters, teenage lesbians, other religious sects like the Children of God – were not being aired anywhere else on television. There was a double stigma: we weren't networked, and our slot at Sunday lunchtime meant we were considered a children's programme. Perhaps a third problem was me – plenty of the critics had loathed me on the radio and they still loathed me on television. But the majority of my viewers did not, and I received plenty of letters and loads of feedback when I went shopping or travelling around London – a surprising number of people seemed to be tuning in.

Although the Moonie film had been well received, secretly I wasn't too happy with our slightly censorious tone. I reluctantly came to the conclusion that groups like this one performed quite a useful function – they soaked up the sads from society and made them feel part of a club or tribe. Over the past few 100 years there had always been fringe religious movements appealing to people who wanted to get away from their lonely souls and families. As long as the disciples didn't feel uncomfortable about handing over their belongings, I couldn't really see what the problem was, if they were over the age of consent. But the generally accepted view – in the press and the other media – was that all sects were inherently bad, run by charlatans. I disagreed, but was in a minority. After the series ended for the summer I took a short break in California and then returned for my acting debut – thankfully Equity had granted me a union card, and I was to be paid the huge sum of £503.50.

In the rehearsal room in the BBC tower building, just round the corner from North Acton tube station, I opened my eyes and scrambled into a chair, clutching a well-thumbed script. Philip Saville's working methods were weird, to say the least. I soon discovered that I had no scenes whatsoever with Donald Pleasence and John Bluthal, and once we had spent a couple of days on read-throughs, we were summoned at different times to work on specific bits of script.

Donald couldn't have been more charming and accommodating on the odd occasions our paths crossed. I asked him how I could learn my lines, as I was having trouble. He told me to recite them into a tape recorder and play the cassette while I was travelling, cooking, doing the ironing. I spent an hour reading out my lines in the bath, and then stuck the tape recorder at the end of the ironing board while I tackled a couple of shirts. The result was horrific – I hated the sound of my voice, and it destroyed what miniscule amount of self-confidence I had managed to muster! After that the whole acting escapade morphed into a chore.

Meanwhile, in Acton, another BBC drama was being rehearsed on a different floor of the building. It was called *I Claudius*, and was rumoured to be full of blood and guts and outrageous scenes of depravity. My old friend John Hurt was starring as the evil Emperor Caligula, but our paths never seemed to cross in the canteen.

The next week I spent several days being filmed cycling around the back streets of Ealing, following a camera mounted on a trailer. This was pretty risky – both for me and for other road users, as I was always hopeless on a two-wheeler and had only had a tricycle as a child. I had to stop at a pre-arranged point, park the bike without it falling over, take my video camera out of the basket, run up a flight of steps, ring a doorbell and deliver some lines. We must have attempted this sequence about fifty times. Philip Saville had the patience of a saint. I could walk, or talk, or cycle, but combining all three eluded me for about two hours until we finally hit the nail on the head.

My part of the drama was being shot with wobbly

camerawork, and was going to be treated afterwards so that it looked like amateur footage. I had to work very hard to remove the constant look of panic from my face. Eventually we finished on location and had two recording days in the studio at the BBC Television Centre in White City. I still couldn't remember my lines, and was sticking them (out of sight of the cameras) all over the set with little arrows telling me where to move next – I'd heard that some of the cast of *On the Buses* did the same thing. In desperation Philip Saville agreed to put some of my script on autocue.

The play was transmitted on BBC2 on 29 September 1976. It was hardly reviewed at all, because at exactly the same time ITV showed a documentary about the Second World War called *The Hunting of Force Z*, made by an award-winning Canadian film-maker (whom I'd never met) called Frank Cvitanovich. *Force Z* grabbed all the attention and the ratings because of the clever way it seamlessly blended archive footage of naval manoeuvres in the Pacific with newly shot dramatic sequences. I wasn't remotely disappointed that my dramatic debut had passed unremarked; at least it meant that I escaped being publicly pilloried about something else.

David Halliwell was disappointed that *Meriel the Ghost Girl* didn't get more attention, especially as Philip Saville's production had used so many bold techniques. Donald Pleasence left the country a week after we'd finished in the studio, to shoot a film in Israel, and I didn't see him again before his death in 2006. But Halliwell was keen to work with me on another project. We co-wrote a proposal for a television drama series about Sheila Garrett, a young woman who worked as a television presenter and came from a working-class background. In our outline she went from writing a newspaper advice column to presenting a radio show and then a television series in which she gave out advice. But fame and success brought all sorts of drawbacks, and the ordinary people who loved her so much because they felt she was one of them became intrusive. She became a drunk and her show was cancelled – she was back on the scrap heap, condemned to being ordinary. It was called *The People's Voice* and, besides using stuff that had happened to me, was inspired by the success of people like Anna Raeburn, who was very popular on Capital radio in London. I was very interested in the rise of agony aunts and sex therapists, both on the radio and in numerous women's magazines. It was a new kind of journalism, with a new cast of pundits and 'experts'.

David was dead keen that I should play the main part, but I had real reservations. He wanted to write another part for me in a play he was working on called *Blood Relations*, to show the doubters that I could act. I knocked that idea on the head straight away. Then I had a phone call from the playwright Alan Plater, who wanted to know if I would play myself in a television drama series he was writing. I immediately declined – I knew my limitations. I had enjoyed working with David Halliwell, though, because I was fascinated by the whole concept of celebrity and fame, and how television was throwing up new kinds of heroes and creating new stars from people with working-class backgrounds. We finished our outline and had meetings with various producers at the BBC and ITV, but nothing came of the idea. Halliwell and I went our separate ways, and I embarked on another series of documentaries for *The London Weekend Show* – I felt much more at ease being myself on camera, rather than a fictional character devised by someone else.

Chapter 10

In late 1976 I was making an episode of *The London Weekend Show* in the studio on the South Bank, about the latest outrageous hair styles, with about half a dozen people known as the Bromley Contingent (some of whom became the band Siouxsie and the Banshees) and they had brought along a surly young man called Sid Vicious. His companions had blue, black, spiky, mohican and real works of art on their heads, but his own hair seemed just filthy and dishevelled. He was pallid, spotty, skinny, wearing a ripped-up T-shirt and a padlock through the crotch of his trousers. With the explosion of musical styles, from punk to rockabilly, more and more people were experimenting with wild colours and haircuts – it was another way of expressing your individuality.

I was gathering confidence about interviewing people on location, but I was still rather nervous in the studio. Mr Vicious looked like big trouble. He hawked up a large amount of phlegm from his throat and spat it on the floor. Next, he lit a cigarette. I was told to rehearse my introduction to the programme, which was on autocue in front of this bunch of sneerers, and I was sweating with nerves. Sid started mimicking me every time I spoke, and in the end I totally lost it and told him to shut up (to 'fucking well shut up', to be precise).

Soon Gerald Chambers, the patronising studio floor manager (who wore an immaculate navy-blue blazer, grey flannel trousers and a white hankie in his breast pocket) appeared. My heart sank, now I had well and truly lost my grip on the situation. 'Look here, Sonny Jim,' he boomed at Sid Vicious, 'you know the rules. Get that cigarette out of your mouth, sit up and stop swearing, otherwise you're out of here.' Astonishingly, it worked. Sid stubbed his fag out on the floor and from that moment on was completely pliant. He didn't say much of note, but at least the gobbing stopped.

Afterwards, Andy commiserated with me in the bar. I was supposed to be the host of the programme, but it felt almost impossible to get any of the youthful vitality and spirit we captured on film in the grim setting of a television studio. Young people felt intimidated, and who could blame them? Andy and I had been working together for 18 months – he had been my mentor, my guide in the weird world of television where I often felt very ill at ease. I knew I seemed gauche and lacked confidence – strange, really, when outside a studio I was full of opinions and never short of a put-down or two. But walking through a studio, where all the technicians on the floor were men, who seemed to speak to each other in an old-fashioned version of rhyming slang, and who spent every lunchtime in the bar and stuck strictly to their quota of tea breaks, was a daunting experience.

I'd first seen the Sex Pistols at the artist Andrew Logan's studio early in 1976. Andrew was an old friend I knew from the early days of hanging out with Zandra Rhodes, we both wore a lot of his chunky mirrored jewellery and I'd attended his Alternative Miss World contests. This party was on Valentine's night and was in full swing when Tony and I arrived. Andrew lived on the top floor of the Butlers Wharf warehouse building, just downstream from Tower Bridge, across the river from Narrow Street. We climbed the stone stairs and went into a large room with a raised stage and a pool made of plastic in front of it. There had been a bit of a buzz about the Sex Pistols, who'd been playing at small clubs around London. When they took to the stage it was total chaos: they didn't seem to know how to play their instruments and the singer was completely tuneless. Nevertheless, there was a real energy and air of excitement about their brief appearance.

The audience was a mixture of artists like Allen Jones and Doug Field, clubbers like Michael and Gerlinde Kostiff, fashionable hairdressers like Keith from Smile and plenty of curious musicians – among them were Mick Jones, Brian James and Tony James with their manager, Bernie Rhodes. Their group was called London SS, and it was to be very short-lived. Mick went on to form the Clash, managed by Bernie. Brian formed the Damned, who ended up putting out the first punk single, 'New Rose', in October that year. Tony James, who I did not meet that night, went on to found Generation X with Billy Idol. Ten years later, he created a group called Sigue Sigue Sputnik, and after meeting in a television studio in the eighties we ended up in a relationship that lasted five years.

The party was not a romantic occasion in any sense of the word. After less than half an hour the music came to an abrupt end when Johnny Rotten's microphone packed up during his version of the Stooges' 'No Fun'. Soon a fight broke out between the band's roadies and the technicians who had supplied the PA system. Tony and I made our escape. I was curious, though, because the Pistols definitely were exciting and full of high-powered energy – even if they were lousy musicians, that didn't seem to be the point. Before long, I would see them play again at the 100 Club and the Nashville in west London, and not long after that I actually met them.

He sat on the edge of the mattress on the floor. A sleeping bag lay on top of it. The others slumped in a line behind him, leaning against the wall, on piles of bedding and cushions. A stuffed rat flew through the air and narrowly missed my head, landing just by my right hand. I decided to ignore it. The skinny boy with the white pasty skin, a sprinkling of spots ruining its perfection, turned his piercing gaze on the camera, ignoring me. His short hair sprouted upwards in tufts, stiffened with some nameless gunk, and was dyed electric orange.

'So, John, who do you rate as musicians?' I knew the question was pointless before I'd finished it. The cameraman moved closer to that unflinching stare.

'I don't have no heroes, they're all useless,' he replied in a quavering north London accent. My sentiments entirely – Johnny Rotten had hit the nail on the head.

To understand where punk erupted from you have to remember that the Beatles had officially split up for good in 1975. The soft sound of lovers rock began to make the charts, but the biggest band was Queen, with their gloriously over-the-top 'Bohemian Rhapsody', the ultimate in pomp rock. Pub rock, which had been so successfully promoted via the Stiff record label, began to fizzle out. We'd had glam rock in 1974, popularised by the huge success of the musical *The Rocky Horror Show*. Singer-songwriters like Randy Newman, Billy Joel, Elton John and Joni Mitchell all enjoyed huge success, but were popular with people over 25.

Punk captured the imagination of young people because you didn't need loads of money, you could do it

yourself. All over Britain kids ripped up their clothes, stuck safety pins in them, dyed their hair with Krazy Colour and sported mohicans. Politicians like the prime minister Harold Wilson (followed by Jim Callaghan in 1976) and Margaret Thatcher, who had just succeeded Ted Heath as leader of the Conservative Party, seemed from another era. They had zero appeal for anyone under 21. We were experiencing an IRA bombing campaign, with bombs going off in the London Hilton and

Piccadilly, all adding to the feeling that the old values were under threat.

In the summer of 1976, during a break from *The London Weekend Show*, Tony and I went to New York. Among the clubs we visited was one in the Village called CBGB's, where the music was hot and furious – this version of punk was exemplified by bands like the Ramones, who played at the Round House in London in July and were absolutely fantastic. Their album, which had been released at the end of April, contained 14 songs and lasted just 28 minutes – packed with excitement. Kids in the UK read about it in the music press – *NME* regularly reviewed the new bands playing at CBGB's. I had brought back a lot of copies of *Punk* magazine (a well-produced New York based fanzine with letters, reviews and comic strips) together with their T-shirt emblazoned with 'PUNK' across the front in white paint on black.

Gradually punk was taking off in the UK, too, by word of mouth and at very small venues. In the beginning punk groups here had to support pub rock bands – the most popular kind of live music. But the scene was gradually growing, and every time the Pistols played in unlikely places like Middlesborough or Scarborough or

at art-school or college dances, more young people turned up and got the message. At the end of August the Pistols played at a midnight event at the Screen on the Green in Islington, London, together with the Clash, and underground films by Kenneth Anger were shown. By October 1976 the Sex Pistols had gathered a considerable underground following. Bolstered by fanzines like *Sniffin Glue*, a duplicated set of handwritten and badly typed sheets stapled together, more and more young people flocked to see the Pistols, the Clash and the Buzzcocks playing regular gigs at small clubs and student dances.

Mark P had been a bank clerk in Deptford, but had chucked in his job to start *Sniffin Glue*, and I went to interview him in his small office in Dryden Chambers, just off Oxford Street. Malcolm McLaren, the Pistols' manager, had his offices in the same building. Malcolm was someone I really didn't warm to, arrogant, sneering and thoroughly intimidating. He regarded the media as morons he had to denigrate at every opportunity. Mark P was different: engaging, intelligent and easy to talk to. His sidekick, Danny Baker, a Bermondsey lad, helped edit the magazine and was a real motormouth – even I could hardly get a word in edgeways!

At the end of October 1976 we'd started a new series of *The London Weekend Show* and I had begun to make a documentary charting the growth of punk. Hence my attempts to interview John in the squat where the band were staying in Denmark Street.

He was already master of the media put-down.

JSP: What kind of people come to see you?

Rotten: I don't know . . . Just bored people, bored out of their brains with hippies.

JSP: What have you got against hippies?

Rotten: They're complacent.

JSP: What do you think about bands like the Stones?

Rotten: I don't. I don't even consider they're a band, they're a business.

JSP: Supposing your record is a success – which there's a big chance it will be – supposing you make a lot of money, how are you going to be different from the Stones?

Rotten: I don't need a Rolls-Royce, I don't need a house in the country, I don't need to live in France. I'm quite happy as I am.

John Lydon was not yet 20 years old, but already he had perfected the single-minded tactics that would mark him out as easily one of the cleverest and most sophisticated people to emerge from the chaos that was punk. He couldn't sing particularly well. He wasn't even particularly interested in bonking or birds, having told one interviewer that sex was 'nothing more than two minutes of squelching'. But he had star quality in spades.

The following week, at the end of October 1976, we rented a large room belonging to the Notre Dame Church just off Leicester Square and used it to stage a gig featuring the Sex Pistols. The resulting footage was to end up on television screens all around the world. Standing at the back of the Notre Dame hall, I was glued to the spot listening to the racket coming from the stage. The Sex Pistols were thrashing their way through 'God Save the Queen', and the audience was going crazy, leaping up and down, pogoing onto each other at the front. Johnny Rotten fixed them with an intense stare and snarled the lyrics, face contorted with loathing. I knew this was an unforgettable night. Andy stood next to me, grinning from ear to ear. What a coup! All the people we'd filmed over the past few months in the Kings Road and in Malcolm McLaren and Vivienne Westwood's shop Seditionaries were there, dressed up to the nines – Jordan, who worked in the shop, was unmistakeable with her cat's eye make-up.

Over the past few months I'd shot interviews with the

Clash, the Buzzcocks, Slaughter and the Dogs, the Stranglers, Siouxsie and the Banshees. Andy and I had documented a musical revolution happening in clubs and on the streets of London; I'd talked to kids in clubs, cafés, at gigs and at bus stops. At last there was a way for young people to get swept up in something guaranteed to annoy their parents, just as rock 'n' roll had done all those decades before. Punk wasn't just about music, it was a way of life, an attitude, a reaction against the bloated sound of stadium rock and middle-of-the-road pop. It was fast, furious, angry. Most of the press seemed to focus on the negative aspects of punk, but I found it exhilarating, a breath of fresh air at a time when the charts were dominated by dreary artists like Peter Frampton and the big summer hit was the Eagles' 'Hotel California' – mindless, bland music to drive to.

Punk appealed to a generation who did not want to follow their parents into boring repetitive work, and spend years saving for a three-piece suite, a better cooker or a tiny flat in a horrible tower block. In 1976 unemployment benefit was only between £9 and £11 a week and punk offered a way of dressing distinctively on a budget; clothes that were torn and customised with safety pins and badges, hair designed to repel everyone but the committed (vegetable dyes and Krazy Colour meant your hair could be pink, purple or orange). Punks wore rubber fetish clothing, bondage trousers, kilts, stuff that Vivienne Westwood described as 'clothes for heroes'.

As we finished the film about the Sex Pistols, in early November I got married for a second time, to Tony Elliott, at a register office off the Commercial Road near Whitechapel, in the East End. The wedding service was printed on laminated cards in English and Urdu. I wore a shocking-pink Zandra Rhodes soft silk jersey blouse and flowing trousers – all the seams were on the outside. My hair was electric burgundy red. Afterwards we had a big party at Narrow Street.

Two weeks later, on 28 November, my punk film featuring interviews with the Pistols and the Clash was transmitted at Sunday lunchtime – the first time the bands had appeared on television anywhere. It didn't exactly hit the front pages and what few reviews we did get were somewhat patronising. According to *The Times*, 'All art demands order, shape, ritual: punk rock, in its present inchoate state, can only be a transient

phenomenon.' *The Listener*'s critic was even more confused: 'The glamorised pictures of this group [the Sex Pistols] were alarming. But the same boys interviewed backstage seemed crumpled, hurt and on the defensive about their inarticulate songs. I felt that the group were in need of help.' By early December the band had signed to EMI records and released their first single, 'Anarchy in the UK'.

The Sex Pistols' manager, Malcolm McLaren, told interviewers that he was a 'situationist', who had been inspired by the Dadaists and surrealism. He was brilliant at orchestrating stunts, as the next few days would prove. Thames Television had a weekday teatime live chatshow hosted by a middle-aged man, who certainly liked a drink, called Bill Grundy. His researchers had seen my film, and decided to invite the Sex Pistols onto his live show. Naturally, they played up to the cameras, and, spurred on by Mr Grundy's goading, John unleashed a stream of expletives and there was uproar and a huge number of complaints. Now the Sex Pistols made all the headlines – just as 'Anarchy in the UK' went on sale – and the band started a nationwide tour with the Clash and the Damned.

The *Evening Standard*'s banner headline read 'Punks – Rotten and Proud of it!' There were to be many more in a similar vein over the coming months. Pub bands like Kilburn and the High Roads now seemed like yesterday's news. At a time when unemployment was growing and politicians seemed totally out of touch, punk offered a ready-made way to be different from your parents. It was a real generation-divider, just as the Stones' music had been back in the early 1960s and Bill Haley and the Comets and Elvis Presley and Gene Vincent had been in the 1950s.

A new tribe had arrived, with Johnny Rotten its unlikely leader. But it couldn't last. It was bound to auto-destruct.

Postscript

After we'd made 100 episodes, *The London Weekend Show* finally got some decent press coverage with a big feature on the leader pages of *The Times*, together with a picture of me and Johnny Rotten, surely some kind of a first. Up to now the show had been ignored because of its Sunday lunchtime slot and the fact that it only went out in the London area. It had been consistently nominated for awards, but lost out to mainstream factual series transmitted nationwide in the evening.

I spent one awards ceremony in the ballroom of the Hilton sitting an a table with Denholm Elliott and Peggy Ashcroft. Unfortunately, I wore a dress by Zandra Rhodes which consisted of one long piece of fabric wrapped round my body. When I went to the ladies' loo in the interval I had to untie it, and for the life of me couldn't get the bloody thing back on again. Luckily, the musical star Elaine Stritch (who was filming a comedy series, *Two's Company*, for LWT at the time) came to my rescue and attempted to rewind the frock round me. I went into the toilet looking chic and came out looking like a badly wrapped parcel. Back at the table Denholm was looking morose and had spurned his seafood cocktail starter (which came inside a hollowed-out coconut) in favour of a large spliff, which he was happily puffing away at in full view of the cameras. Needless to say, no one on our table won a thing all evening.

During 1977 I made quite a few films about the whole punk phenomenon; the rise of strongly individual women like Poly-Styrene (singer with X-Ray Spex), Vivienne Westwood (who reopened her shop in the Kings Road as Seditionaries, selling to punk acolytes from all over the world) and Siouxsie Sioux of Siouxsie and the Banshees, who told me that her first attempt at singing had involved putting together a medley of 'Twist and Shout', the Lord's Prayer and 'Deutschland über Alles'.

The Sex Pistols topped the British charts in the week

of the Queen's silver jubilee in 1977 with their version of 'God Save the Queen'. There was a hot rumour that the BPI, who compiled the pop charts, were furious and that officially the Pistols had been denied the number-one slot. It was thought to constitute a major embarrassment to the bigwigs in the recording industry, who were all seeking gongs for their contribution to exports and so on. Critics claimed they didn't want to rock the boat.

Tony and I were finding it increasingly difficult to live together. We both had such demanding jobs. We bickered, and he was uncomfortable with all the attention I was receiving from my television work. Whenever we went to a restaurant, he was furious that I could just call up and get a table, but, even though he owned a highly successful magazine, no one knew who he was. It wasn't really my problem, but I could understand it – and I was sick of hearing about the never-ending struggles with the staff on *Time Out*. Nevertheless, we decided to celebrate the jubilee with a two day snooker tournament at Narrow Street, on Monday and Tuesday, 6 and 7 June 1977.

We installed a second snooker table at the river end of our ground floor; the house was perfect for parties: the

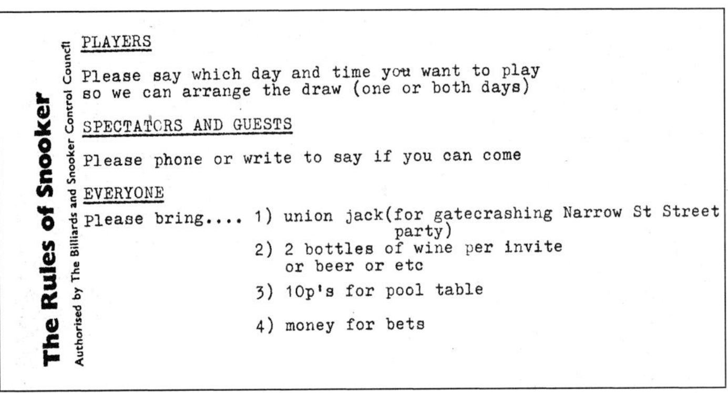
The Rules of Snooker
Authorised by The Billiards and Snooker Control Council

PLAYERS

Please say which day and time you want to play
so we can arrange the draw (one or both days)

SPECTATORS AND GUESTS

Please phone or write to say if you can come

EVERYONE

Please bring.... 1) union jack(for gatecrashing Narrow St Street party)
2) 2 bottles of wine per invite or beer or etc
3) 10p's for pool table
4) money for bets

living room on the first floor was over sixty feet long, with a wooden balcony over the water. I set to and made about 20 pounds of chili con carne, mixing it in the bath. We ordered hundreds of hamburgers from the butchers who supplied the Hard Rock Café. Even my parents were enthusiastic about it – they had high hopes of either my father or my brother-in-law Michael winning.

Around 100 people came, but the trouble was that the players were so keen that they arrived early to practise, well before noon. Someone brought a barrel of real ale, and in the afternoon some non-players were just slumbering on the sofas. My friend Paul had made the most beautiful trophies for the winner, runner-up and highest break. I was very touched when he produced a special one for me, complete with a red haired mini-Janet

standing on a replica table. Andy, Bruce and all the gang from *The London Weekend Show* came, as well as Tony's closest friends (who tended to be the management) from *Time Out*. Old mates like Zandra Rhodes, Dougie Field and Piers Gough, and even Tim Street-Porter, now a friend again, put in an appearance. There was one Canadian man I didn't know. Tony introduced me: he was the Canadian film director Frank Cvitanovich (the man whose film had been transmitted on ITV at exactly the same time as my disastrous dramatic debut in *Meriel*). He was charming, in his late 50s, with long grey hair and a moustache. I didn't know that Tony had once had an affair with Frank's partner Midge, the mother of his son Bunny. In the middle of our tournament I judged the fancy dress competition in the Brightlingsea council flats opposite, and was very glad to see the last snooker player finally depart around 1 a.m. on day two!

Next day, Tony slept off a hangover while I washed the kitchen floor. I'd had enough. We had a blazing row and decided to separate, when my TV series had ended, in order to attract minimum publicity. It wasn't that we didn't get on – we just could not live together with the careers we were both totally committed to pursuing. Eventually he moved out, saying he was going somewhere where 'room service didn't answer back', which turned out to be the Holiday Inn in Swiss Cottage.

A year later, in July 1978, *The London Weekend Show* finally came to an end after over 150 editions over a period of nearly three years. I had started my career in television as a complete novice, and now I wanted to move out of the restrictive arena of youth programming and into the mainstream as a presenter. Once again John Birt was to plot my next career move, as a co-host with Russell Harty and Clive James of a late-night satire show for LWT, which would air only in the London area. My working relationship with Andy had come to an end.

By now the long hours and the lunchtime drinking were really taking their toll. Both Andy and Bruce were substantial drinkers, but I couldn't function in the afternoons if I downed vodka and tonics at midday. I decided to stop drinking completely, and didn't touch a drop for several months. I lost weight, I looked great, but it was bloody hard work and pretty boring. And because I'd never drunk Coke or sweet fizzy drinks there was absolutely nothing except tonic water I could touch instead; there was no alcohol-free lager in those days. When I decided to start drinking again, I went to the pub across the road from London Weekend with Andy one evening. Two beers and I was completely pissed – how did these men do it?

Gradually Andy and I drifted apart as I worked on *Saturday Night People*, and then an early evening series *The Six O'Clock Show* with Michael Aspel. Andy seemed relegated to being one of a large team of producers, not really at ease. We'd had some great times, but once we stopped filming documentaries our relationship was never the same, and we drifted apart now that we no longer spent five days a week together.

Punk didn't last much longer than my marriage. By the end of 1978 Tony and I were divorced, and the Sex Pistols had split up. One day, Tony telephoned to say he'd thought of someone who was perfect for me – he reintroduced me to Frank Cvitanovich, who I eventually married. A new era was beginning both at work, and at home.

List of Illustrations